AMERICAN LETTERS

works on paper

giovanni singleton

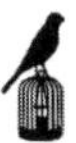

CANARIUM BOOKS
ANN ARBOR, MARFA, IOWA CITY

SPONSORED BY
THE HELEN ZELL WRITERS' PROGRAM
AT THE UNIVERSITY OF MICHIGAN

AMERICAN LETTERS

works on paper

Canarium Books
Ann Arbor, Marfa, Iowa City
www.canarium.org

The editors gratefully acknowledge the
Helen Zell Writers' Program at the University of Michigan
for editorial assistance and generous support.

Cover: giovanni singleton, *temptation*.

Design: Joshua Edwards

First Edition

Printed in the United States of America

ISBN 13: 978-0-9969827-6-4

Thank you Mom (Candace Brown), grandmom (Carrie B. Neal), Ronaldo V. Wilson, Judy Halebsky, Carmen Giménez Smith, Brenda Hillman, Jeroline Harris, Tiffany Higgins, Douglas Kearney, Evan Lavender-Smith, devorah major, Douglas "D. Scot" Miller, E. Ethelbert Miller, Toi Derricotte, Michelle Bradshaw, Gloria Frym, Laurie Ramey, Phyllis McEwen, Sarah Menefee, Patricia Dienstfrey, George Mattingly (GMD Design), Aldon Nielsen, Denise Newman, Gloria Jean Walker, Amarnath Ravva, opal palmer adisa, and Kathy Evans for your invaluable support and dynamic presence on the planet.

Additionally, UC Berkeley's 2017-18 Holloway Lectureship in Poetry allowed me to get a much needed catalytic converter for my car, among other things, and provided me with a rare and precious, stress-free respite in which to finally gather these pages. I also extend a deep, eternal bow of gratitude to Canarium Books for their generous attention and kind efforts which made this book possible.

for

Julie Ezelle Patton

&

Christine Wertheim

CONTENTS

CHAPTER 1

exhibits

In an attempt to document a lineage of African American and African Diasporic avant-garde/experimental/oppositional writing, I have constructed these three poems (a flag, a cross, and a blank page) using the Library of Congress card catalog numbers (archival finds) for works that in one way or another exemplify just such a lineage. These three "gatherings" are also an attempt, via the visual ordering, to (re)situate this lineage within the context of so-called "American Letters" which at times has denied its existence, rendered it invalid, and/or relegated it to the margins.

EXHIBIT A

American Prose

[PR9320.9.H3C3][PS153.N5M24][PS3563.A3166D53]
[PZ3.D3923BE5][PR9320.9.H3R47][PZ4.M652Fr]
[PZ4.R82254Or][PS3555.V34G6][PZ4.H318As]
[PS3563.A39A45][PS3562.0442L5]

[PS3563.A3166B4][PS3561.E392D5][PS3561.E3717A82][PS508.N3c66]
[PS3560.0483M67][PS3555.V34Z8][PZ4.K285Du][PZ4.K285De]
[PZ4.57276Le][PZ4.M23A][PS3553.A7736227][PZ4.J7553]

E X H I B I T   B

American Poetry

[PR9272.9.C54D6][PS3529.D44T5]
[PS3570.H568B3][PS3563.U3954T75]
[PS3558.U46766A89][PS3553.072S25]
[PS3561.E423T5][PS3570.H568C5]
[PS3553.072C6][PS3573.R5364A6]
[PR9230.9.B68A6][PS3568.0235W5]
[PS3552.A583R4][PS3561.A84G6]

[PS3560.076A63][PS3562.04418J8][PS3554.U43P6][PS3563.C3872B53]
[PS3551.T55H4][PS3558.U46766L6][PS3568.0235E8][PS3557.I78G57]

E X H I B I T C
American Letters

CHAPTER 2

cagedbird

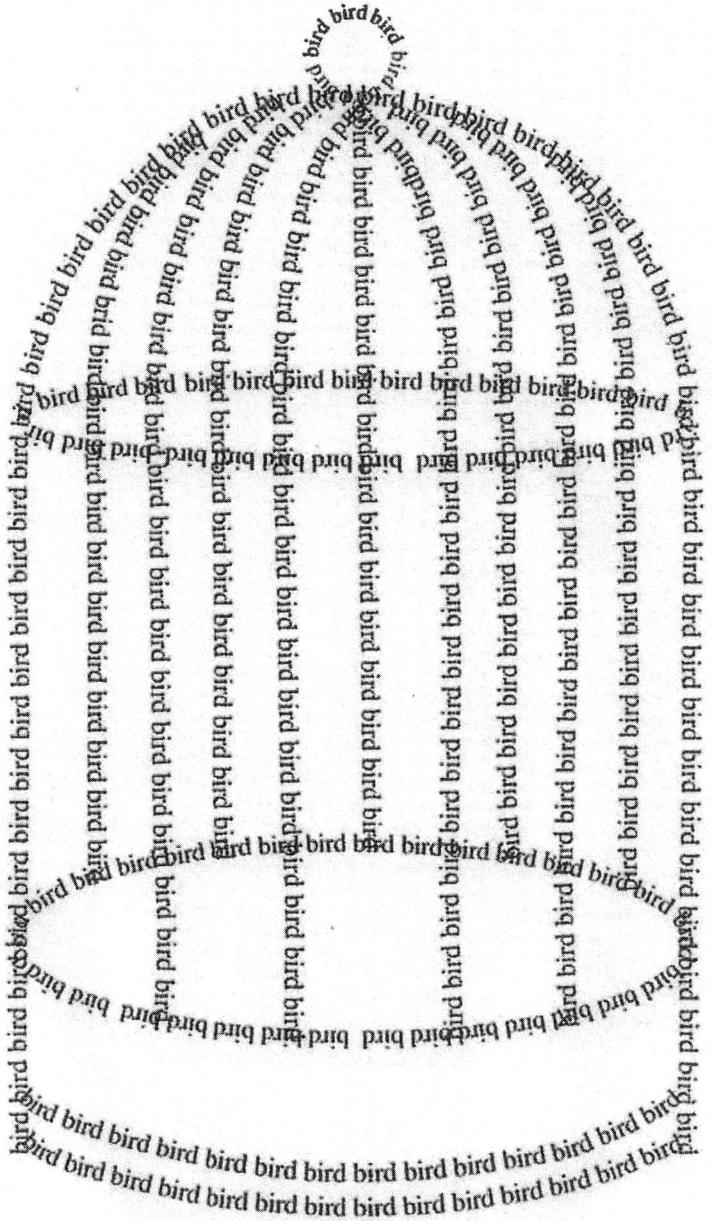

bird bird bird

bird bird bird bird bird bird bird bird bird bird bird bird bird

bird bird bird bird bird bird bird bird bird bird bird bird bird bird

bird bird bird bird bird bird bird bird bird bird bird bird bird

bird bird bird bird bird bird bird bird bird bird bird bird bird

PERFORMANCE SCORE for *cagedbird*

bird bird *Ju Ju* bird drum bird Charlie bird Parker bird i'm for the
bird bird Ju Ju bird drum bird Charlie bird Parker bird im for the
birds not the cages people put them in bird john john bird cage bird
birds not the cages people put them in bird john john bird cage bird
conference of the birds bird bird *Gets The Worm* bird sheltering sky
conference of the birds bird bird Gets The Worm bird sheltering sky
bird bird bird bird say bird fly bird land bird bird bird song song *Fine*
bird bird bird bird say bird fly bird land bird bird bird song song
and Dandy bird sky sheltering bird bird bird *All the Things You Are*
Fine and Dandy bird sky sheltering bird bird bird All the Things
bird bird *East of the Sun* start again bird parker bird Charlie bird
You Are bird bird East of the Sun start again bird parker bird
Parker come come together birds *Uptown* stellar jay bird wings
Charlie bird Parker come come together birds Uptown stellar jay bird
spread bird bird red bird bird bird bird feathers bird bird *Oop Bop*
wings spread bird bird red bird bird bird bird feathers bird bird Oop
Sh'Bam bird breathe bird bird b - i - r - d *Ornithology* i'm for
Bop Sh'Bam bird breathe bird bird b - i - r - d Ornithology im
the birds not the cages not the cages not the cages we put them in bird
for the birds not the cages not the cages not the cages we put them
bird not the cages we are in feed bird fly bird free bird live bird live
in bird bird not the cages we are in feed bird fly bird free bird live
bird away bird bye bye black bird
bird live bird away bird bye bye black bird

breeeeeeeeeeeeeathe

breeeeeeeeeeeeeathe

* Every occurrence of "bird" acts as a site for improvisation.

outside is enough to

touch and be free

the farthest edges of human speech
and wilderness unfurl from ruffled

sleep with plans for positioning
laundered lives on display

attendant in open air prayer
so nothing surpasses belief or

declaration of war or tongues
cloaked in broken rot

to meet meaning some form of "we"
are not biodegradable or advisable

how many inscriptions and nouns
come to believe only themselves

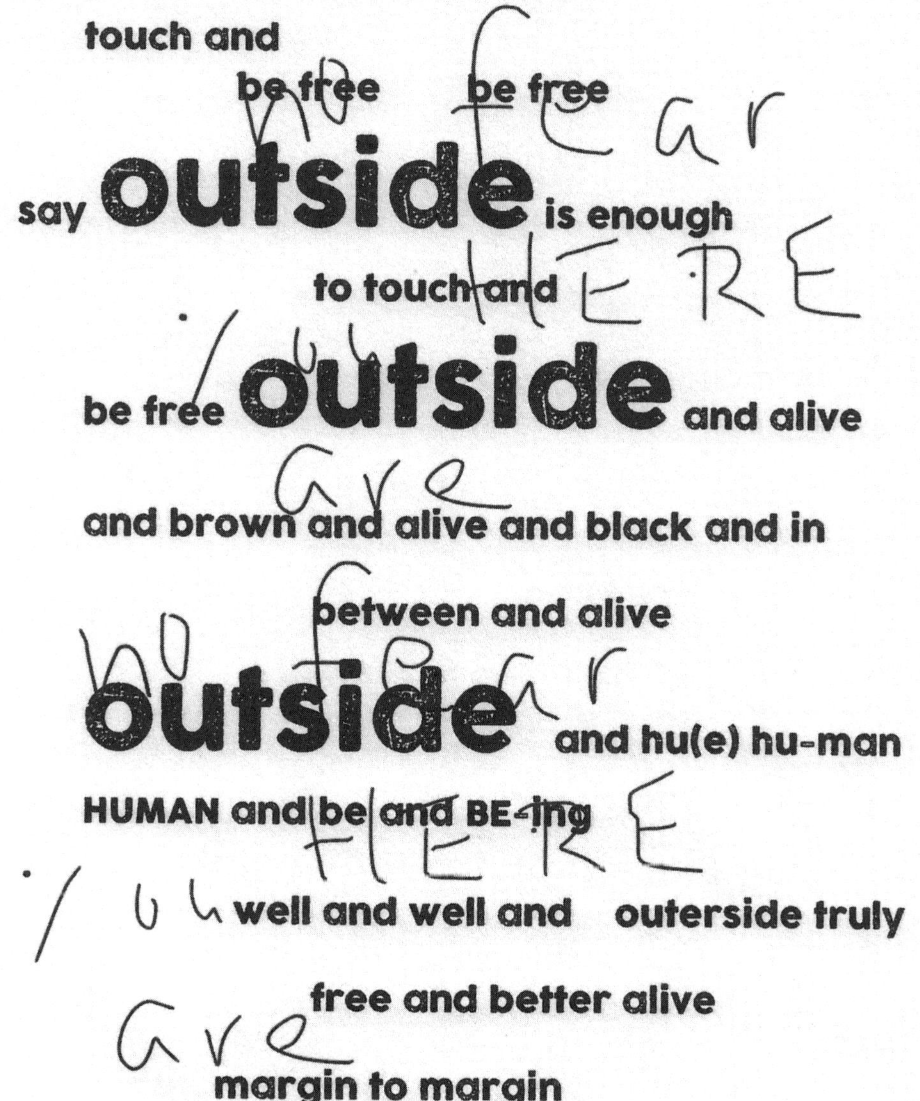

outside is enough to

touch and

be free be free

say **outside** is enough

to touch and

be free **outside** and alive

and brown and alive and black and in

between and alive

outside and hu(e) hu-man

HUMAN and be and BE-ing

well and well and outerside truly

free and better alive

margin to margin

AMEN.

CHAPTER 3

worldview(s)

worldview

I.

II.

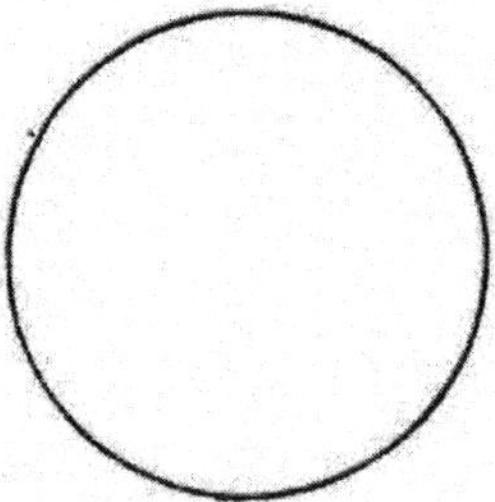

III.

Aaaaah.

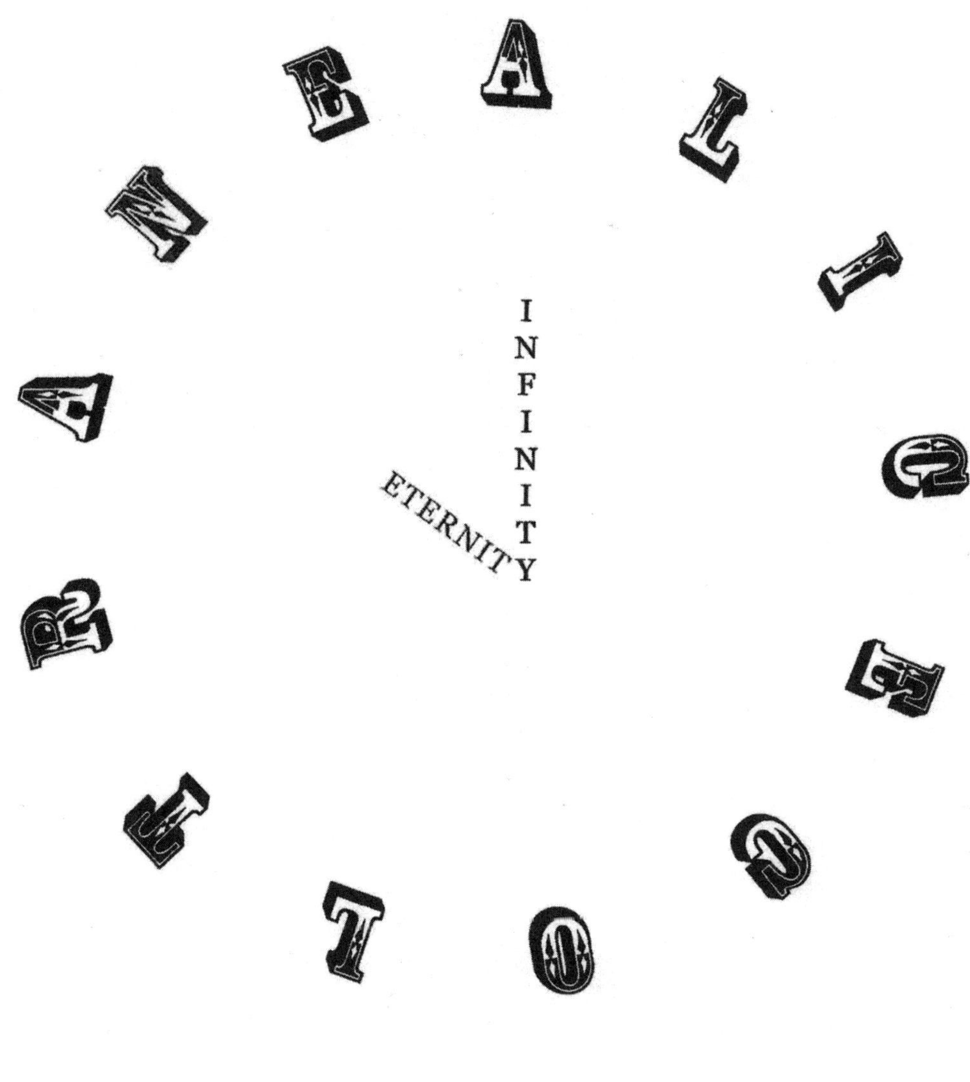
INFINITY
ETERNITY

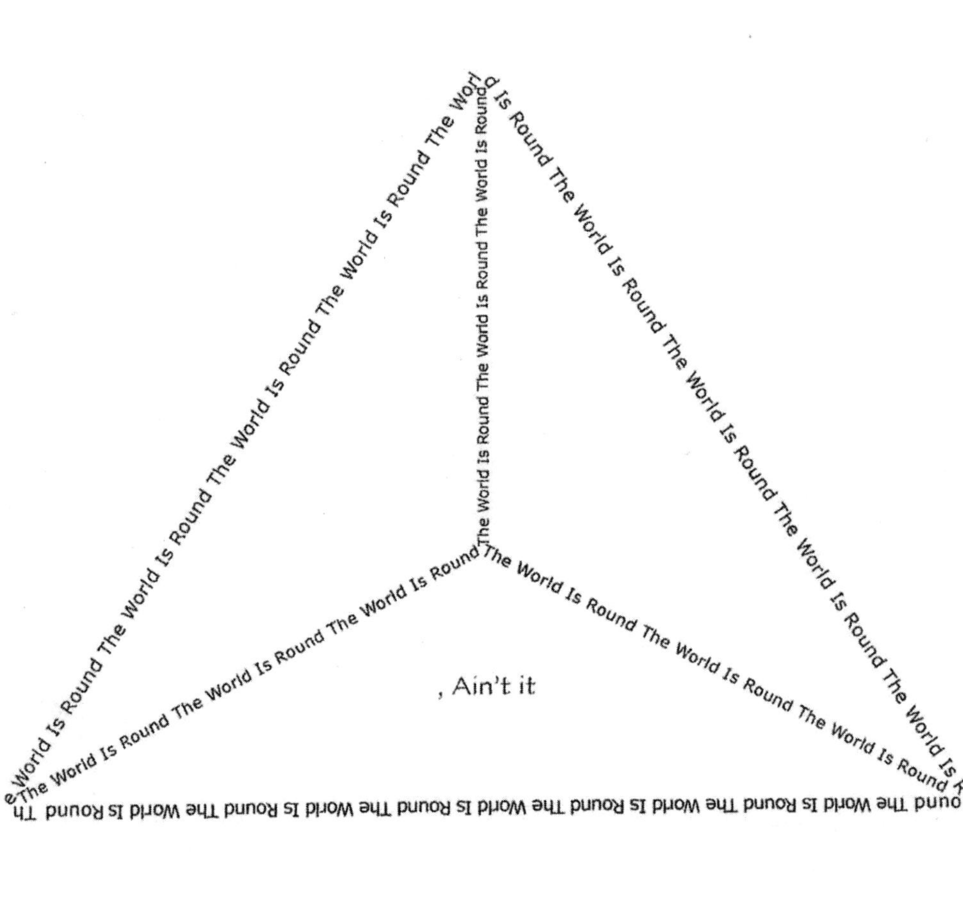
e World Is Round The World Is Round The World Is Round The World Is Round The Worl
d Is Round The World Is Round The World Is Round The World Is Round The World Is R
The World Is Round The World Is Round The World Is Round The World Is Round
The World Is Round The World Is Round The World Is Round
The World Is Round The World Is Round The World Is Round
ound The World Is Round The World Is Round The World Is Round The World Is Round The World Is Round Th
, Ain't it

shuffle the cards lay the runes write some poems and pray pray pray read the leaves roll the dice
shuffle the cards lay the runes write some poems and pray pray pray read the leaves roll the dice
shuffle the cards lay the runes write some poems and pray pray pray read the leaves roll the dice
shuffle the cards lay the runes write some poems and pray pray pray read the leaves roll the dice
shuffle the cards lay the runes write some poems and pray pray pray read the leaves roll the dice

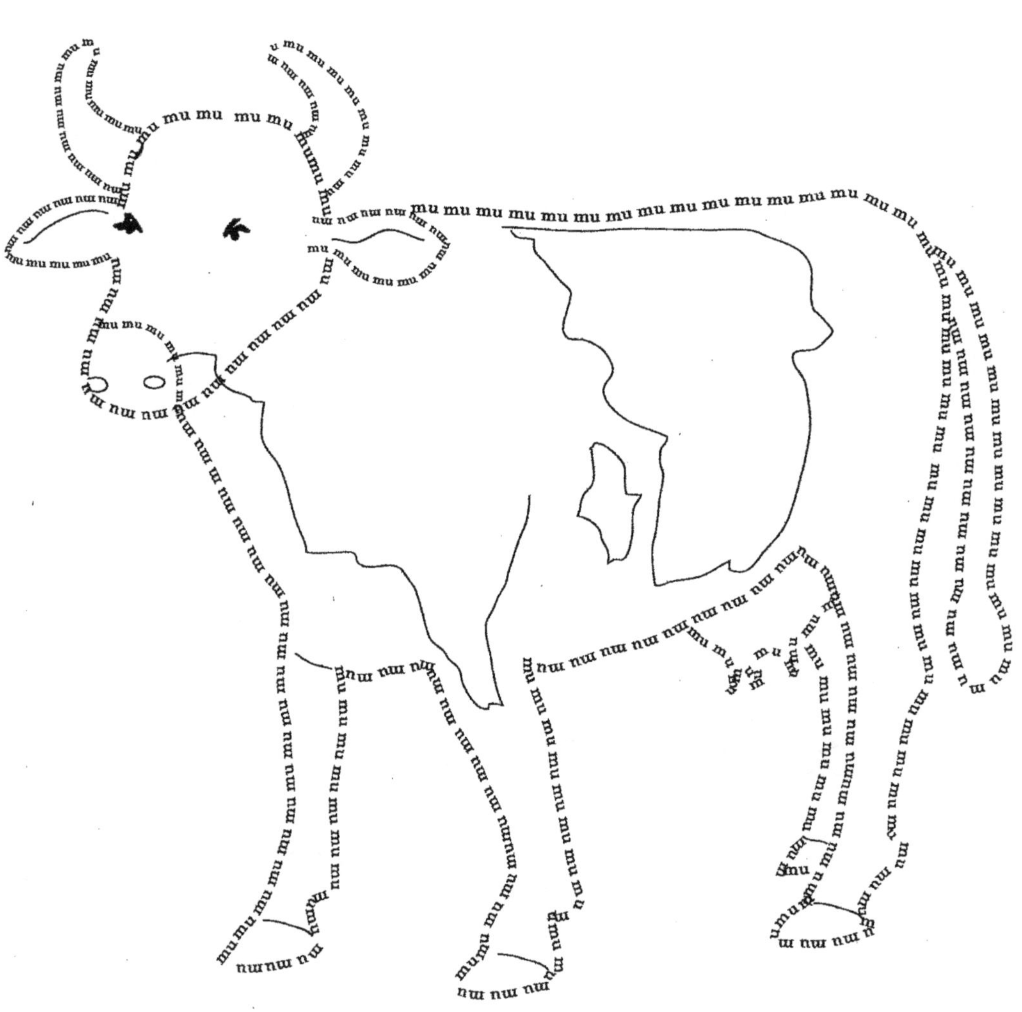

mu	mu	mu	mu	mu	mu	mu
no	no	no	no	no	no	no
not	not	not	not	not	not	not
does a dog	does a dog	does a dog	does a dog	does a dog	does a dog	does a dog
mu	mu	mu	mu	mu	mu	mu
does a dog	does a dog	does a dog	does a dog	does a dog	does a dog	does a dog
mu	mu	mu	mu	mu	mu	mu
does a dog have	does a dog have	does a dog have	does a dog have	does a dog have	does a dog have	does a dog have
Buddha	Buddha	Buddha	Buddha	Buddha	Buddha	Buddha
mu	mu	mu	mu	mu	mu	mu
nature	nature	nature	nature	nature	nature	nature
nonbeing	nonbeing	nonbeing	nonbeing	nonbeing	nonbeing	nonbeing
mu	mu	mu	mu	mu	mu	mu
without	without	without	without	without	without	without
mu	mu	mu	mu	mu	mu	mu
does a dog	does a dog	does a dog	does a dog	does a dog	does a dog	does a dog
have Buddha	have Buddha	have Buddha	have Buddha	have Buddha	have Buddha	have Buddha
nature	nature	nature	nature	nature	nature	nature
study the way	study the way	study the way	study the way	study the way	study the way	study the way
nature	nature	nature	nature	nature	nature	nature
without	without	without	without	without	without	without
mu	mu	mu	mu	mu	mu	mu
does a cow	does a cow	does a cow	does a cow	does a cow	does a cow	does a cow
does a cow have	does a cow have	does a cow have	does a cow have	does a cow have	does a cow have	does a cow have
Buddha	Buddha	Buddha	Buddha	Buddha	Buddha	Buddha
mu	mu	mu	mu	mu	mu	mu
nature	nature	nature	nature	nature	nature	nature
mu	mu	mu	mu	mu	mu	mu
does a cow have	does a cow have	does a cow have	does a cow have	does a cow have	does a cow have	does a cow have
have Buddha	have Buddha	have Buddha	have Buddha	have Buddha	have Buddha	have Buddha
nature	nature	nature	nature	nature	nature	nature
mu	mu	mu	mu	mu	mu	mu
cow	cow	cow	cow	cow	cow	cow
mu do you	mu do you	mu do you	mu do you	mu do you	mu do you	mu do you
do you	do you	do you	do you	do you	do you	do you
mu	mu	mu	mu	mu	mu	mu
do you have	do you have	do you have	do you have	do you have	do you have	do you have
Buddha	Buddha	Buddha	Buddha	Buddha	Buddha	Buddha
mu nature	mu nature	mu nature	mu nature	mu nature	mu nature	mu nature
do you have	do you have	do you have	do you have	do you have	do you have	do you have
do you have	do you have	do you have	do you have	do you have	do you have	do you have

* Every occurrence of "mu" acts as a site for improvisation.

inner/outer ringing
(to be heard)

Some wearing out and leaning forward into
binoculars of Borges' blinded eyes. Time is a
warship. Improved sight in a 20/20 mandala.
The not "I" dream-sees a world in four + plus
directions, circular and miraculous ever-living
so far as in and about and. . .

CHAPTER 4

canon fire :: cosmic clay to be colored

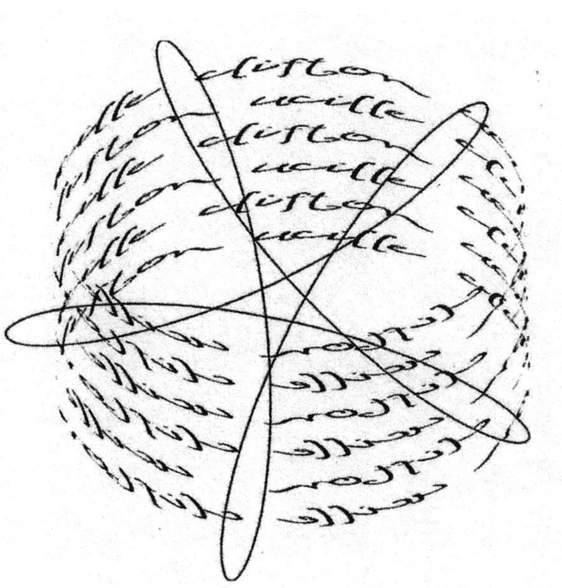

Alice Coltrane: a mesostic

vedAntic

templLe prayers

tamborInes and

hallelujah Claps for

krishna, ganEsha, shiva

turiya's sCripture a

jOurney in satchidananda

beLoved john's

sTained glass face

chuRched in

gospel hArp lord of lords

detroit miNistry pours from

swami's wurlitzEr

Sun Ra Arkestra: a mesostic

aStro black
proUd
fiNs, flesh

and cRown
subliminAlly

trAnsmit
puRple
peeKaboo
interstEllar
chantS
faiThfully
thRough
mAitreyan verse

sanctified: a mesostic
after nina simone

borN to blues
hell raIsed to
an awful straNge pitch
of rAge but

don't let me be miSunderstood
baptIsmal backlash
and oh Mississippi,
gOddam
all these maNy
bluEs still to shout

Bob Kaufman: a mesostic

invisiBly
crOwded
Beatitude

shaKes up
improv jAzz
solitUde
sidewinds aFter
ghostly Minds convulse
on brooding sidewAlks
over Northbeach

Golden Sardine: a mesostic
after Bob Kaufman

amonG
terra cOtta
riddLes
anD a
flutEd
visioN

bliSter
mAdness
coloRs the
sounD of
a nIght poet's
boomeraNg
voyagE

Second April: a mesostic
after Bob Kaufman

wrinkled wallS of
nEgro suits are
transluCent and
prOsaic
iN
gabarDine

zulu lAughter hides
in triPle tones of
ash-smeaRed jazz
and dIluted maroon
gLaciers

The Ancient Rain: a mesostic
after Bob Kaufman

ancienT
wHirlwind
facEs

Above
suN
bleaChed
sphInx and
bluE
volcaNic
deaTh

chambeRs
illuminAte
jupIter's feverish
daNce

CHAPTER 5

illustrated equations

illustrated equation no. 1

something about a look. . . something about seeing. . .

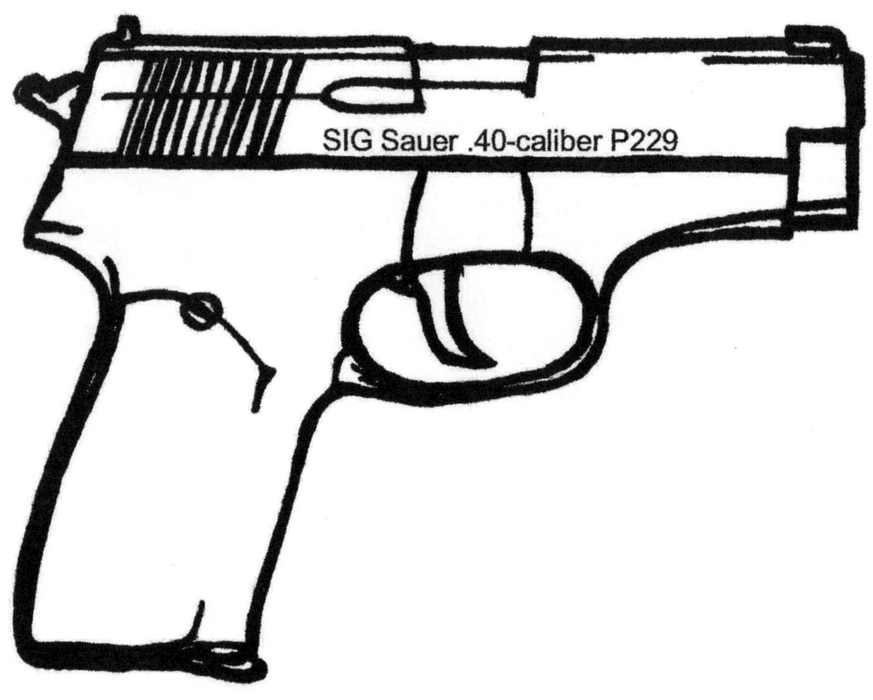

don't

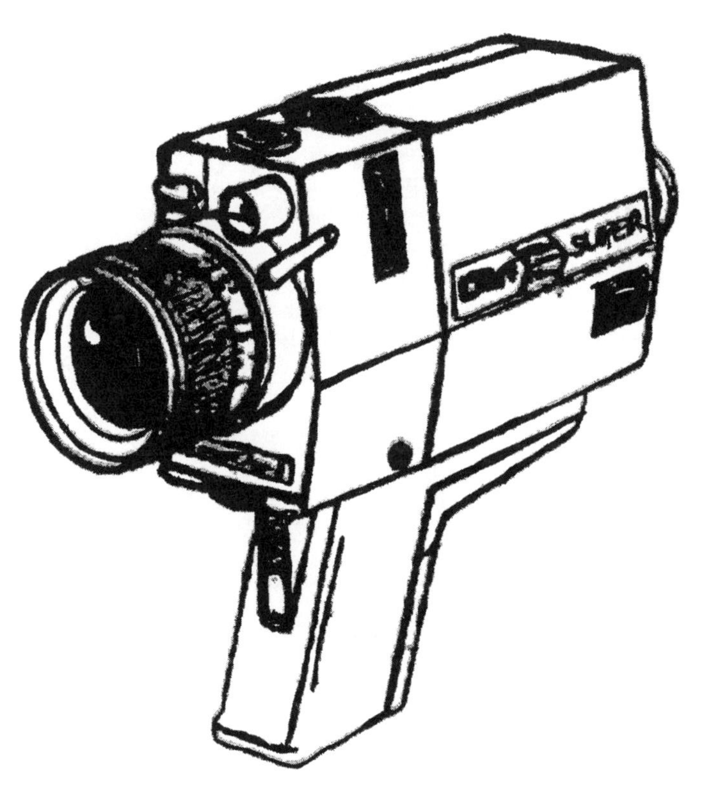

shoot

PERFORMANCE SCORE for *illustrated equation no. 1* (an improvisation)

snap shot
shoot a scene
shoot your mouth off
shoot footage
cell phone   body cam
shooter of the video
the one who shot the video
surveillance   surveillance
head shot
9•1•1 What's your emergency?
a shot in the arm
shoot for the stars
shoot up/shot up/shot down
please state your emergency
take a shot
another shot please
foul shot
double shot   triple shot express-o
United States of America, what's your emergency?
hot shot   big shot   good shot
Emergency, i seen him do it
camera shot
shooter   shoot him   shoot her
sir, turn around and get down on your knees
hook shot
shot her   shot him
ma'am please put down your weapon
film shoot
take your best shot

take my hand
let me stand
hear my call
lest i fall

moonshot
one   last   shot

so get up stand up
stand up for your life
say get up stand up
stand up for your life. . .

illustrated equation no. 2
something about a look. . . the shape of things. . .

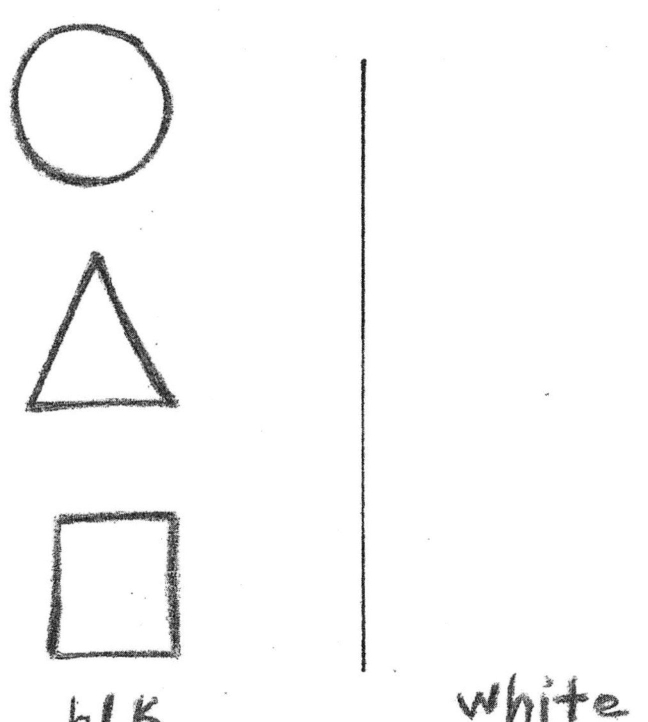

there a boat. there a pair
of oars for moving to and
from shore.

blue breaks down. ghosts
emerge from the river,
manifest as fever and fear.

illustrated equation no. 3
dialogue

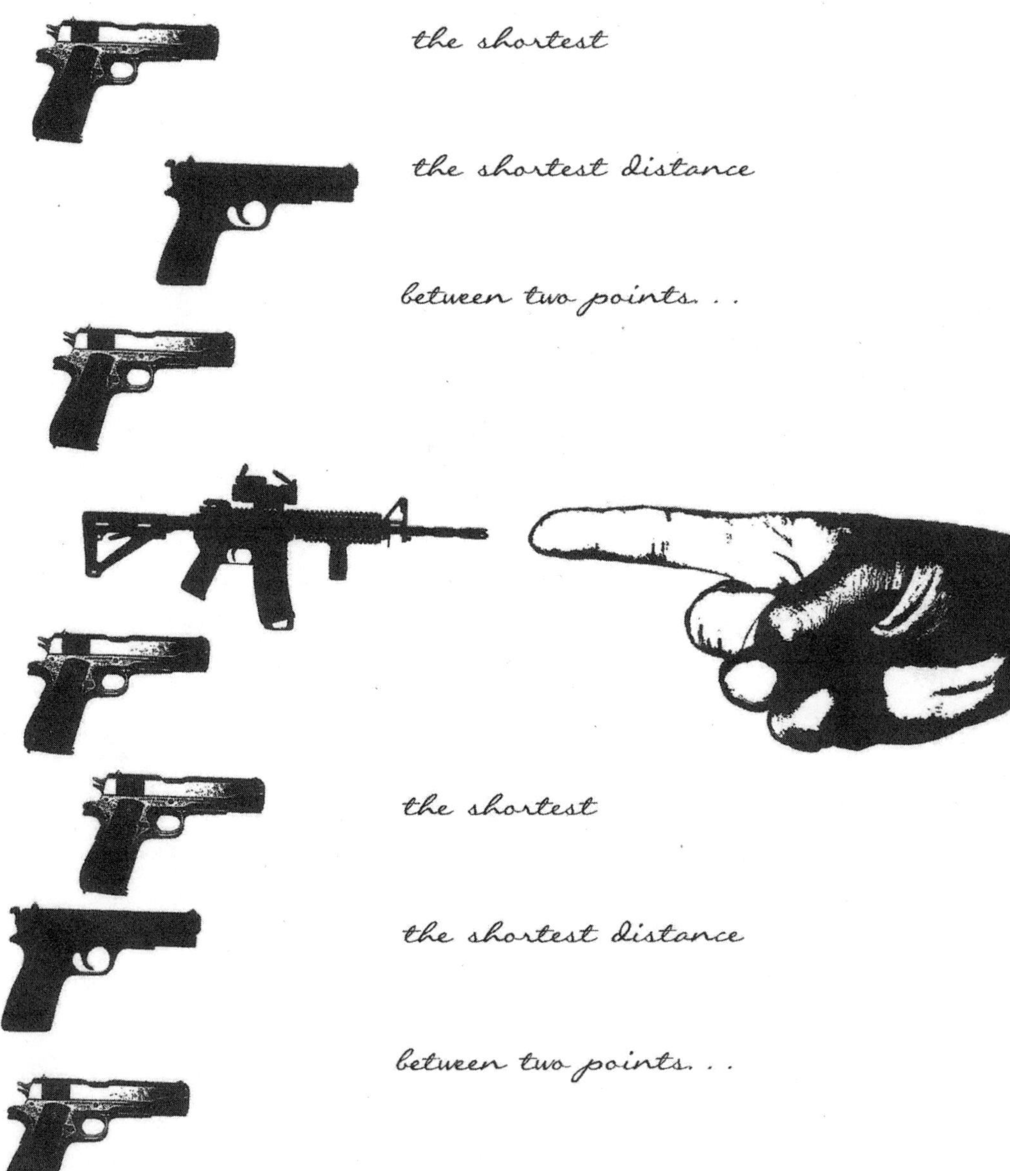

blk $\sqrt{\text{white}}$

square root no. 1

blk + white = blk **AND** white

Things are not as they seem, nor are they otherwise. ~ Lankavatara Sutra

numbers

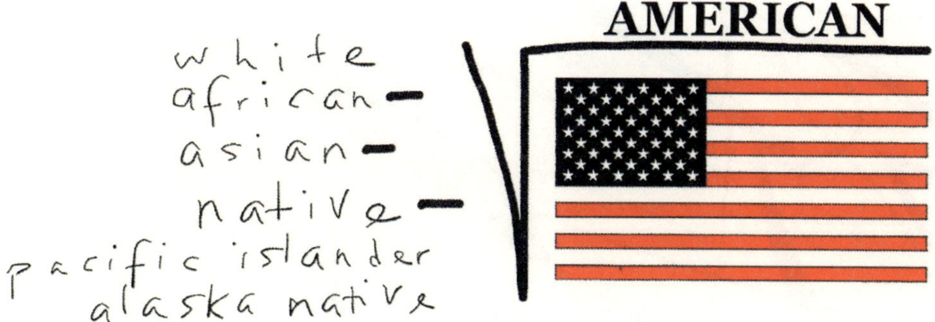

square root no. 2

* The U. S. Census Bureau "collects racial data in accordance with guidelines provided by the U. S. Office of Management and Budget (OMB), and these data are based on self-identification." (www.census.gov)

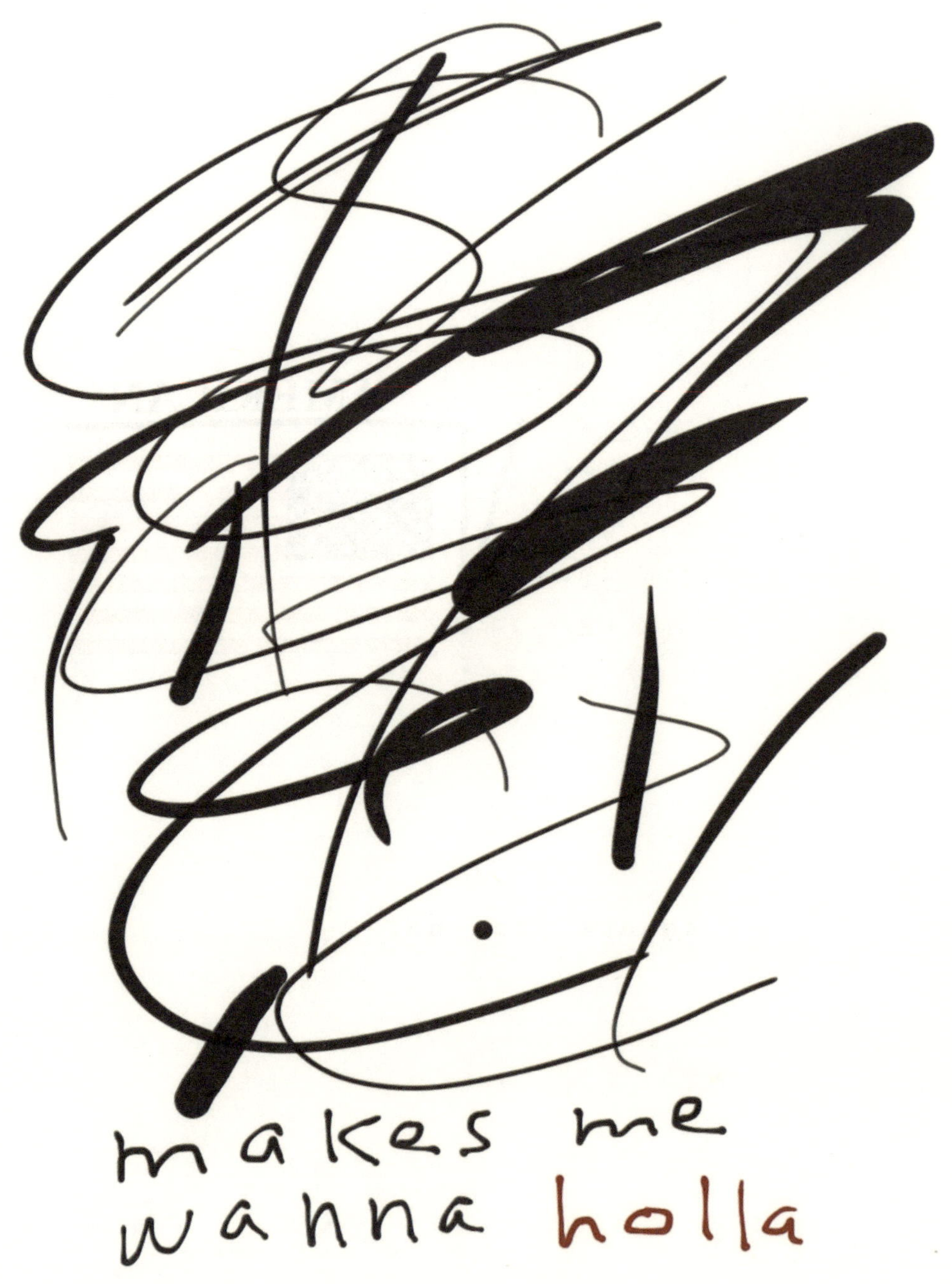

* a line from Marvin Gaye's "Inner City Blues" lyrics

CHAPTER 6

Black Sisyphus - Take the High Road (a quadriptych: presently)

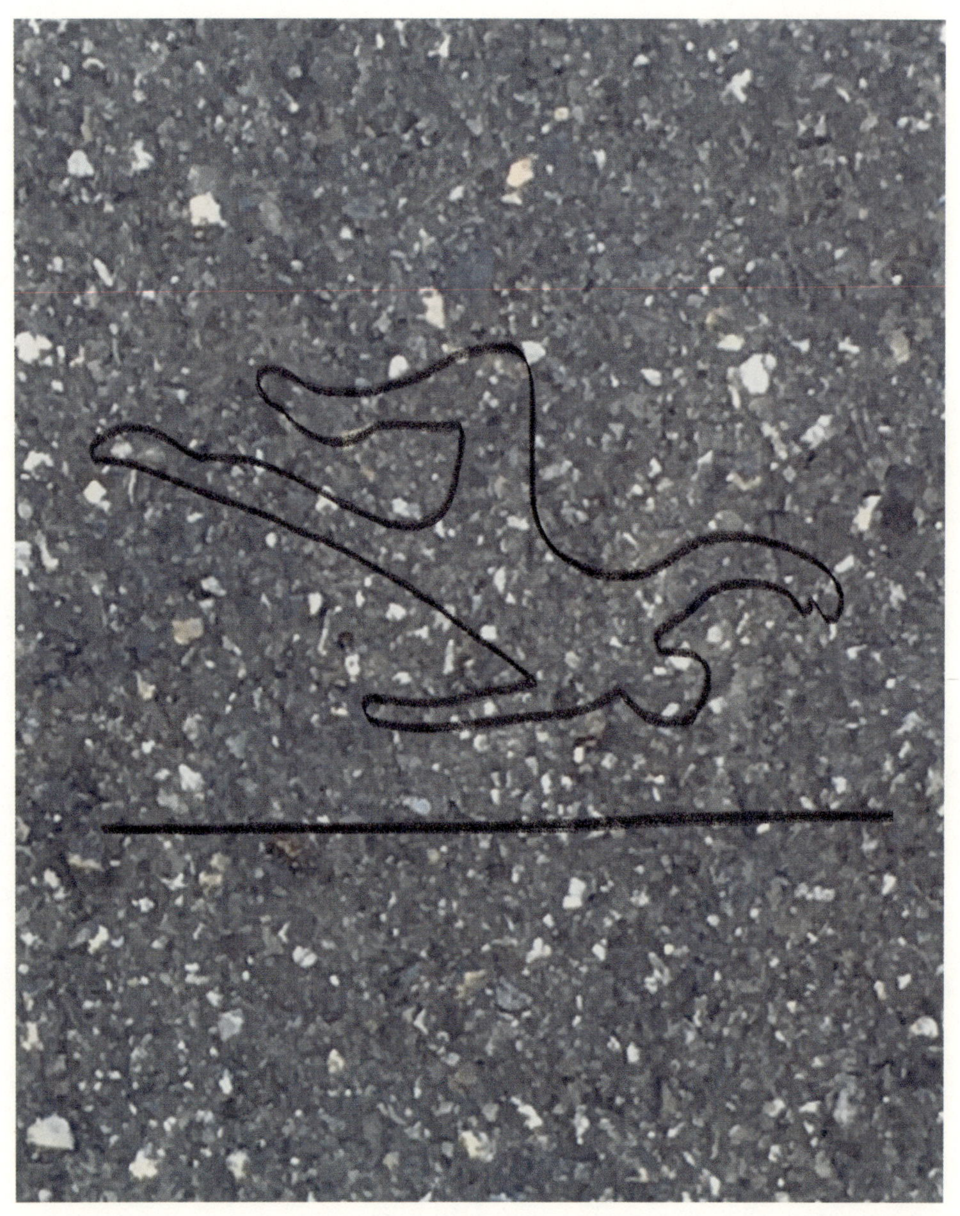

no. 1

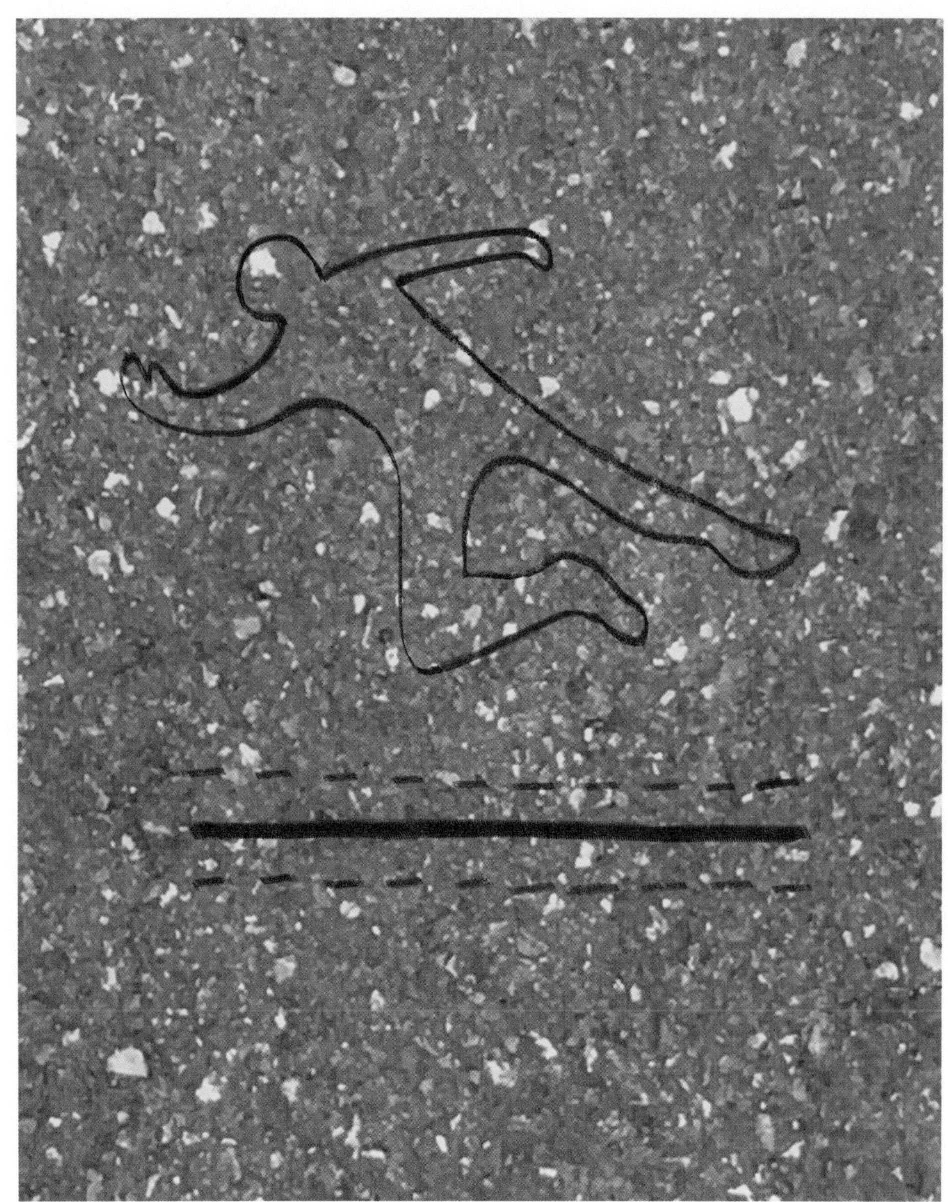

no. 2

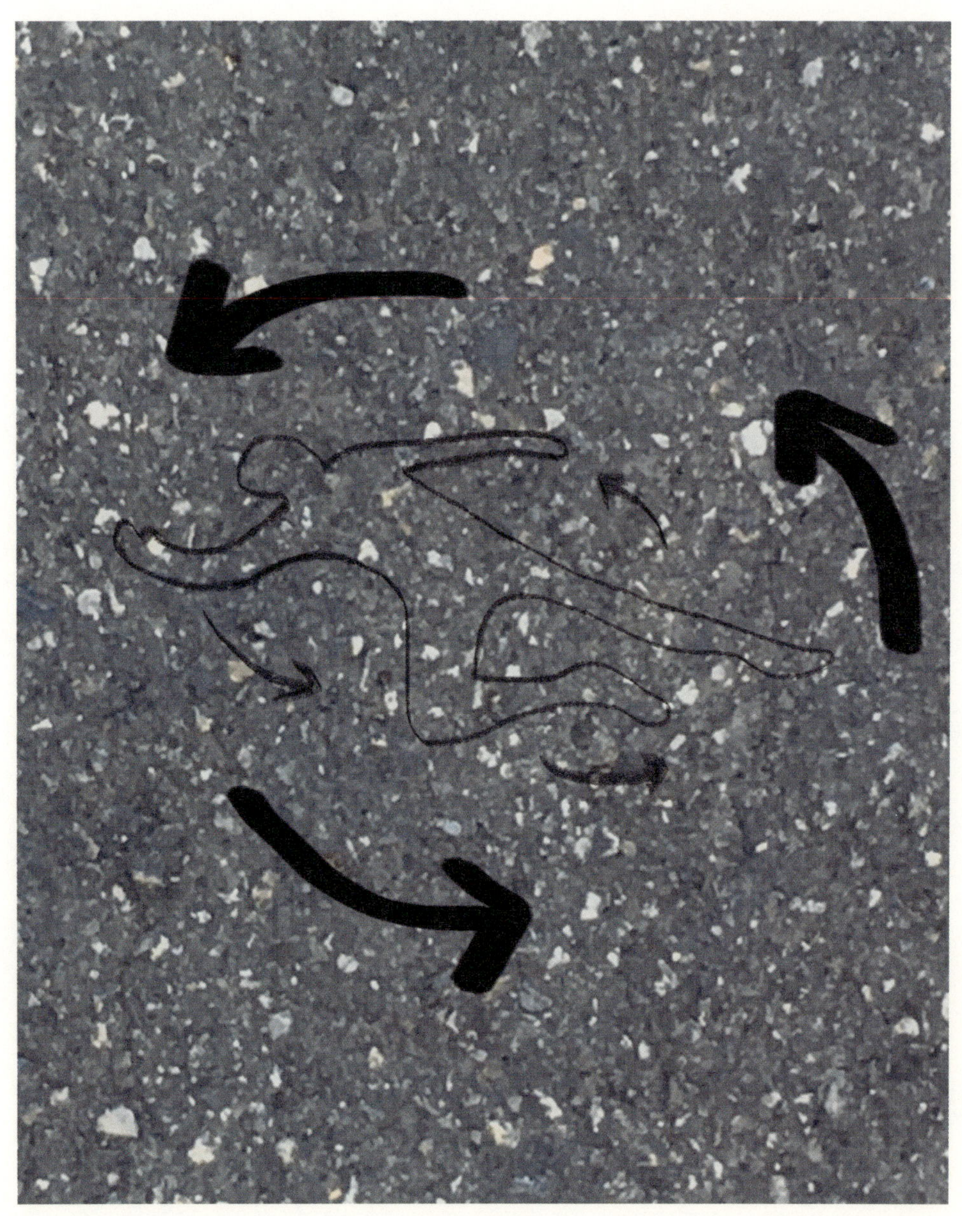

no. 3

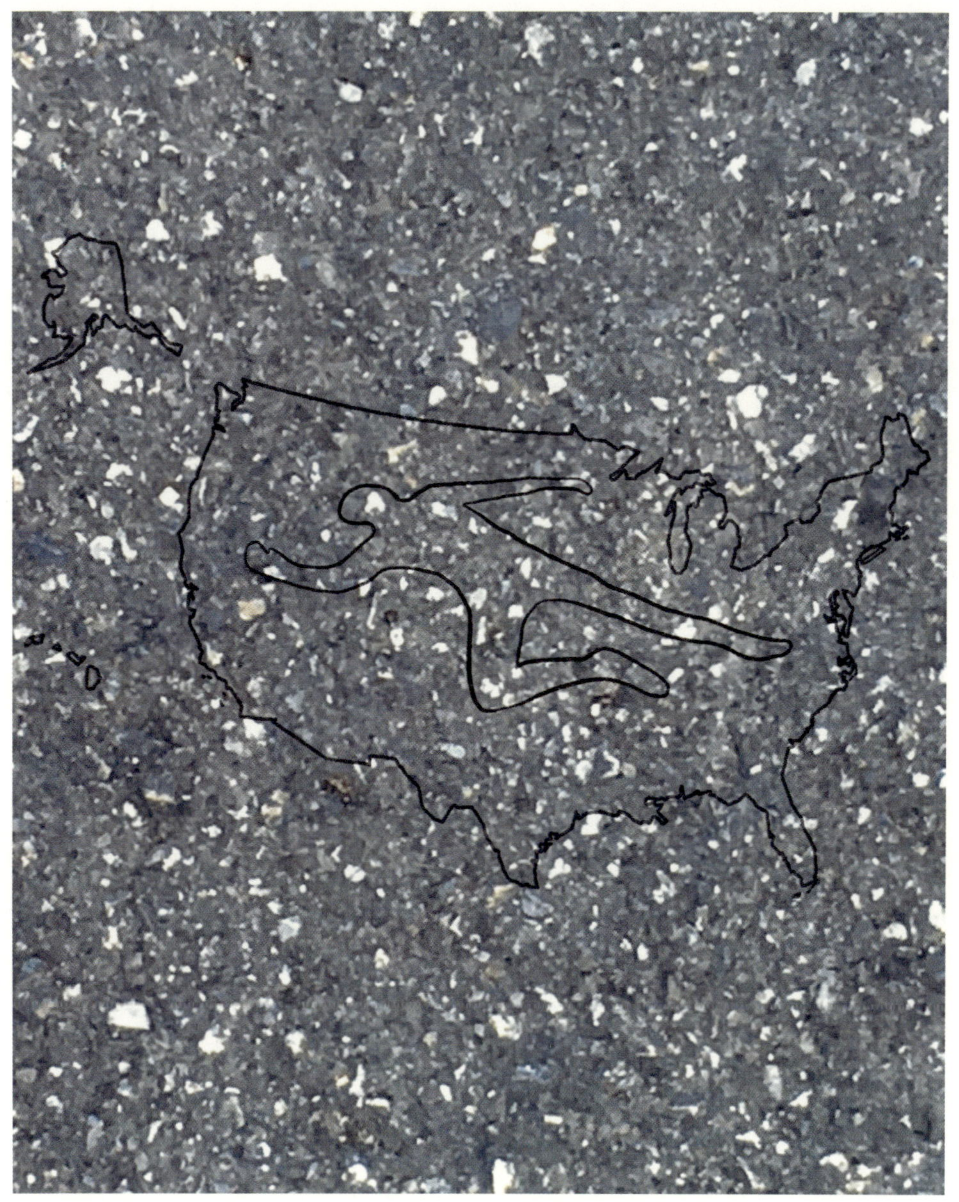

no. 4

CHAPTER 7

olive branches

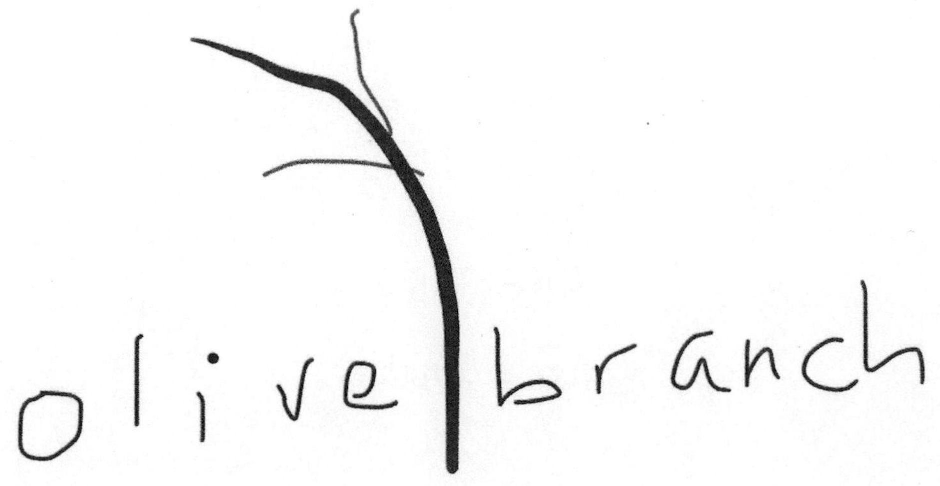

olive branch
no. 1

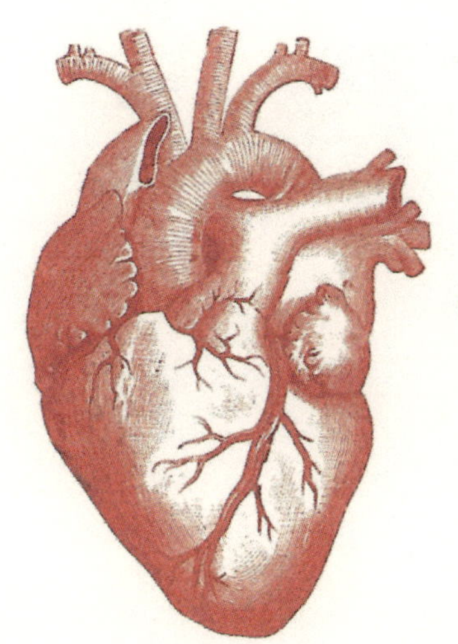

olive branch
no. 2 (too)

olive branch
no.. 2 (too)

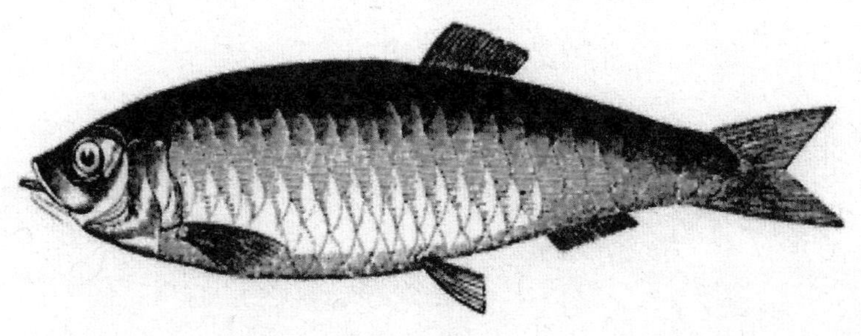

olive branch
no. 3

olive branch no. 37

CHAPTER 8

(k)not-trees

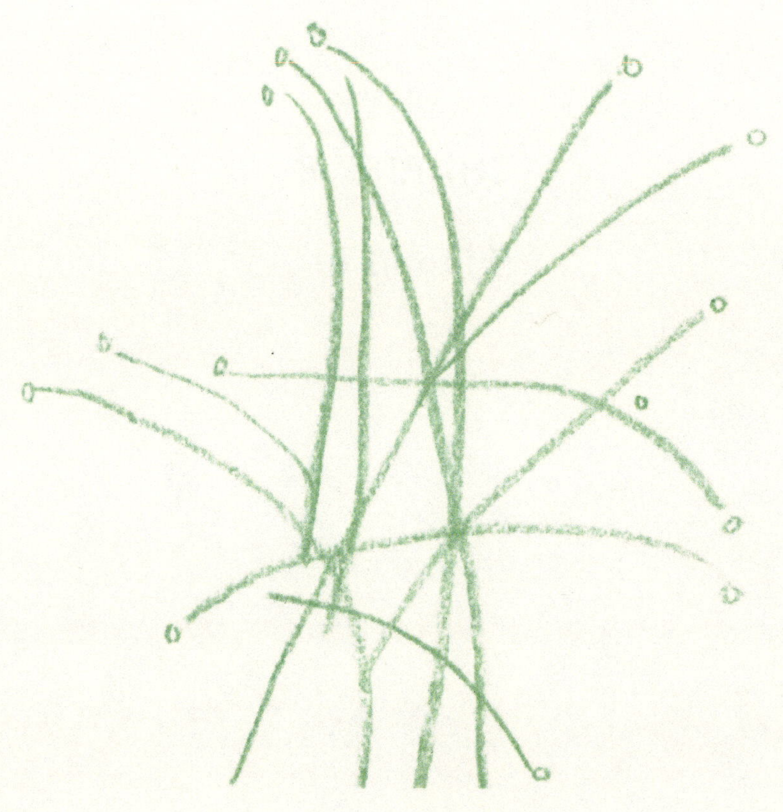

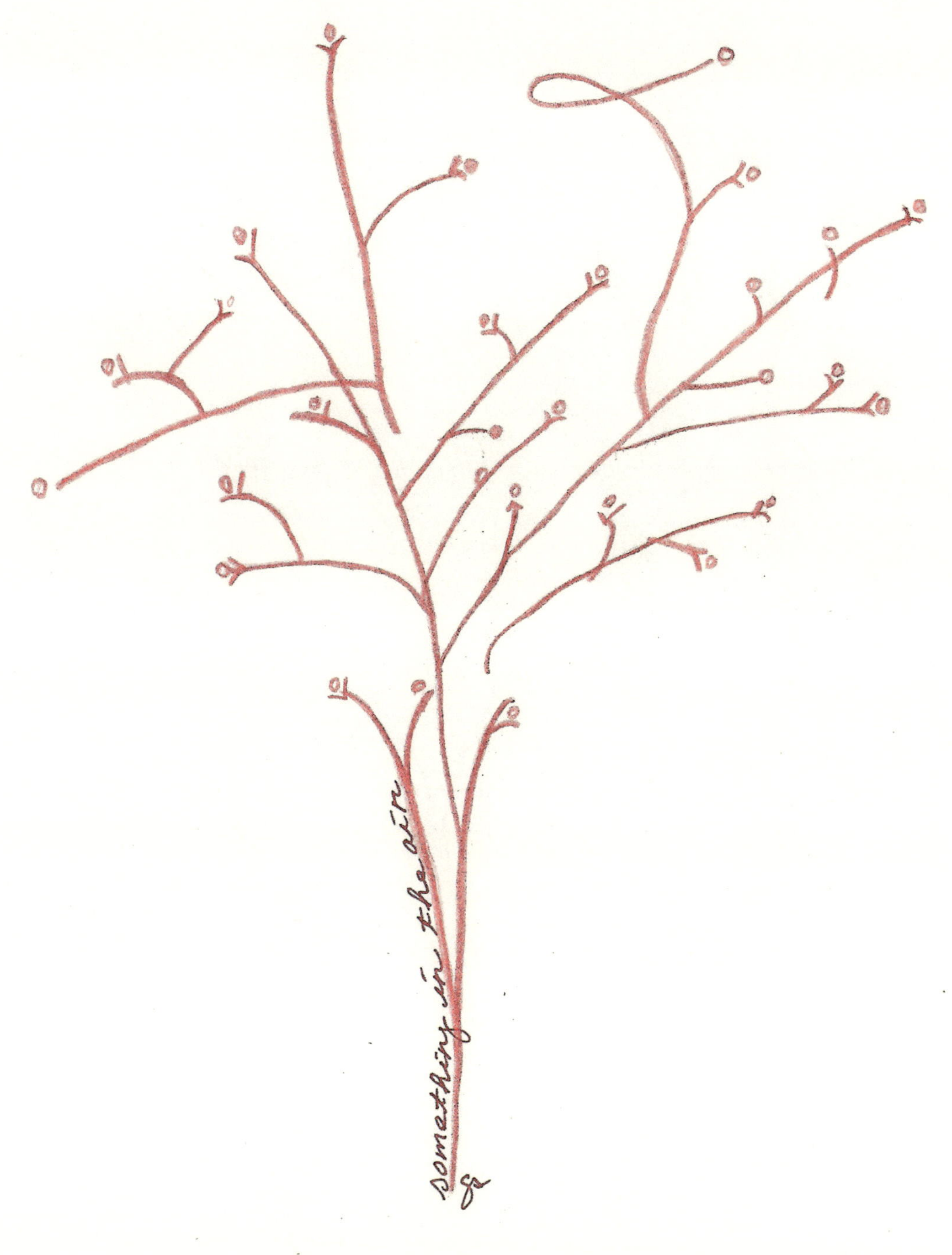
Something in the air

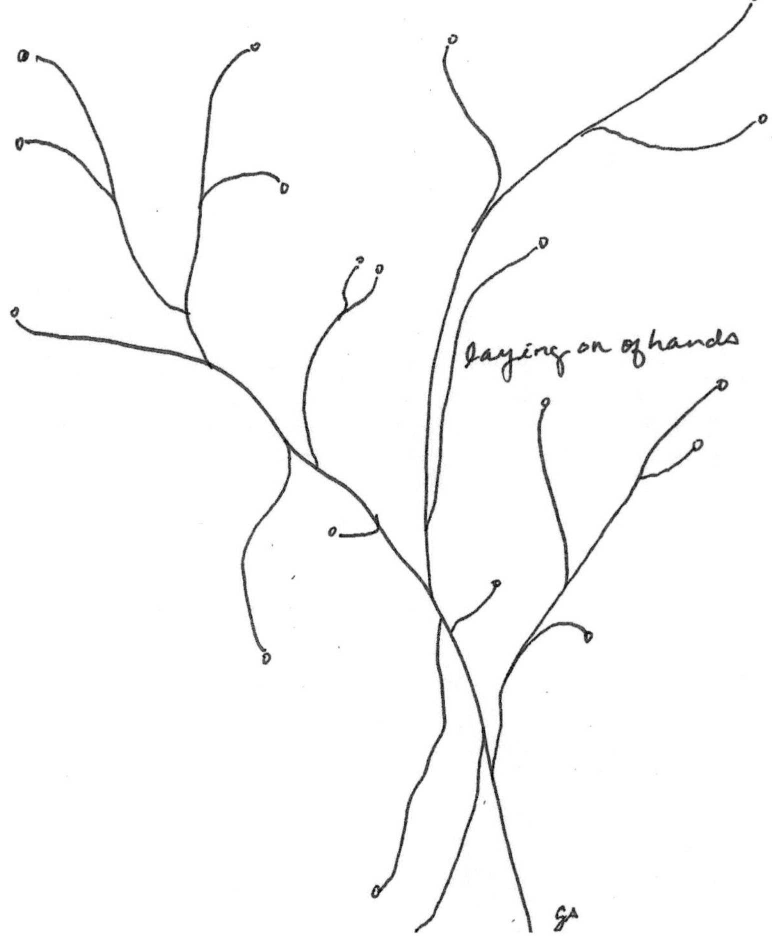
laying on of hands
GA

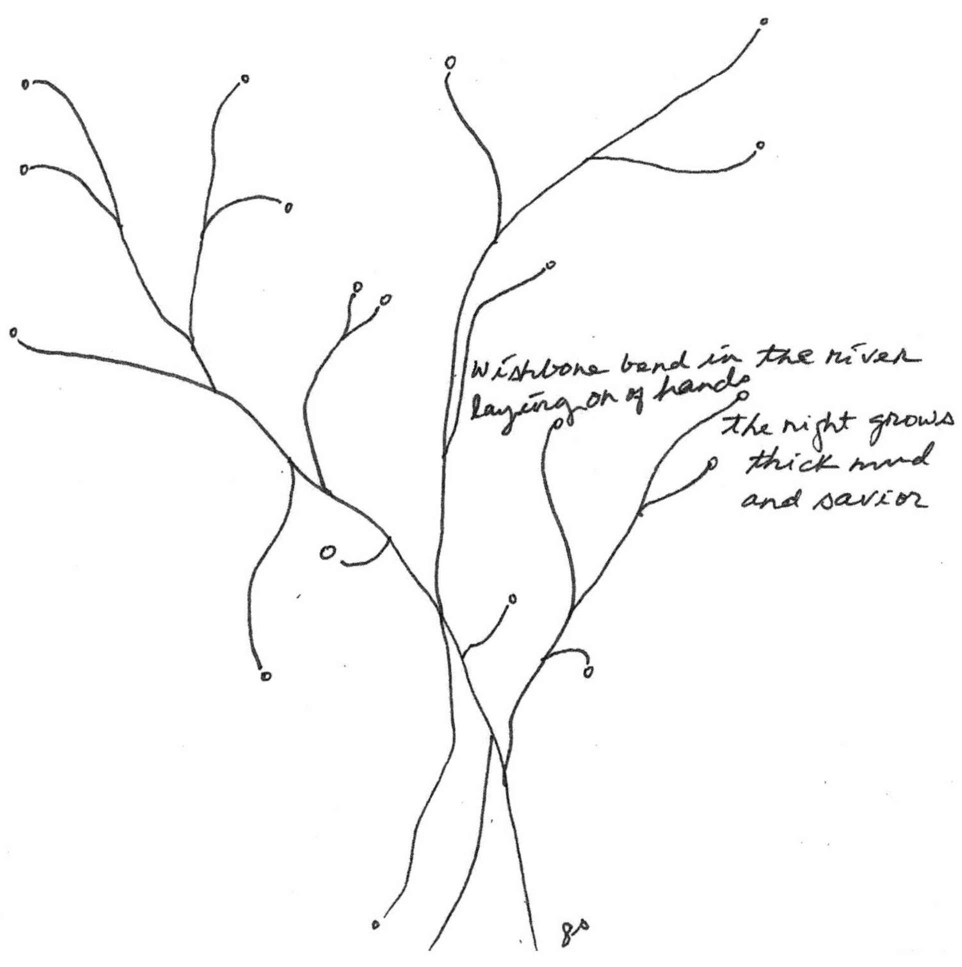
wishbone bend in the river
laying on of hands
the night grows
thick mud
and savior
80

silver tree

for Phebus Etienne

winged traveler keeps watch.
heart in bloom. what was dreamt
of. what we each can only know
for ourselves. bees in their hives.
tempered flame. honey in
glass jars. laughter. gazing that.
often prayer. constellations in a
book. after. wishing still that you
had not gone. after. reflection.
the back/side of it. persistent
wind. time does not answer. its
mouth too much of straw.

CHAPTER 9

rooted

ddd

DA

Actual size: 1 x 2

DA
DA

Actual size: 3 x 3

dadadadadadadadadadadadadadada
dadadadadadadadadadadadadadada
dadadadadadadadadadadadadadada
dadadadadadadadadadadadadadada
dadadadadadadadadadadadadadada
dadadadadadadadadadadadadadada
dadadadadadadadadadadadadadada
dadadadadadadadadadadadadadada
dadadadadadadadadadadadadadada
dadadadadadadadadadadadadadada
dadadadadadadadadadadadadadada
dadadadadadadadadadadadadadada
DADA
dadadadadadadadadadadadadadada
dadadadadadadadadadadadadadada
dadadadadadadadadadadadadadada
dadadadadadadadadadadadadadada
dadadadadadadadadadadadadadada
dadadadadadadadadadadadadadada
dadadadadadadadadadadadadadada
dadadadadadadadadadadadadadada
dadadadadadadadadadadadadadada
dadadadadadadadadadadadadadada
dadadadadadadadadadadadadadada
dadadadadadadadadadadadadadada
dadadadadadadadadadadadadadada
dadadadadadadadadadadadadadada
dadadadadadadadadadadadadadada

Actual size: 3 x 5

daddaddaddaddaddaddaddaddaddaddaddy
daddydaddydaddydaddydaddydaddydaddy
daddydaddydaddydaddydaddydaddydaddy
daddydaddydaddydaddydaddydaddydaddy
daddydaddydaddydaddydaddydaddydaddy
daddydaddydaddydaddydaddydaddydaddy
daddydaddydaddydaddydaddydaddydaddy
daddydaddydaddydaddydaddydaddydaddy
daddydaddydaddydaddydaddydaddydaddy
daddydaddydaddydaddydaddydaddydaddy
daddydaddydaddydaddydaddydaddydaddy
daddydaddydaddydaddydaddydaddydaddy
daddydaddydaddydaddydaddydaddydaddy
daddydaddydaddydaddydaddydaddydaddy
daddydaddydaddydaddydaddydaddydaddy
daddydaddydaddydaddydaddydaddydaddy
daddydaddydaddydaddydaddydaddydaddy
daddydaddydaddydaddydaddydaddydaddy
daddydaddydaddydaddydaddydaddydaddy
daddydaddydaddydaddydaddydaddydaddy
daddydaddydaddydaddydaddydaddydaddy
daddydaddydaddydaddydaddydaddydaddy
daddydaddydaddydaddydaddydaddydaddy
daddydaddydaddydaddydaddydaddydaddy
daddydaddydaddydaddydaddydaddydaddy
daddydaddydaddydaddydaddydaddydaddy
daddydaddydaddydaddydaddydaddydaddy
daddydaddydaddydaddydaddydaddydaddy
daddydaddydaddydaddydaddydaddydaddy
daddydaddydaddydaddydaddydaddydaddy
daddydaddydaddydaddydaddydaddydaddy
daddydaddydaddydaddydaddydaddydaddy

DADDY

Actual size: 4 x 6

DAD

Actual size: 5 x 7

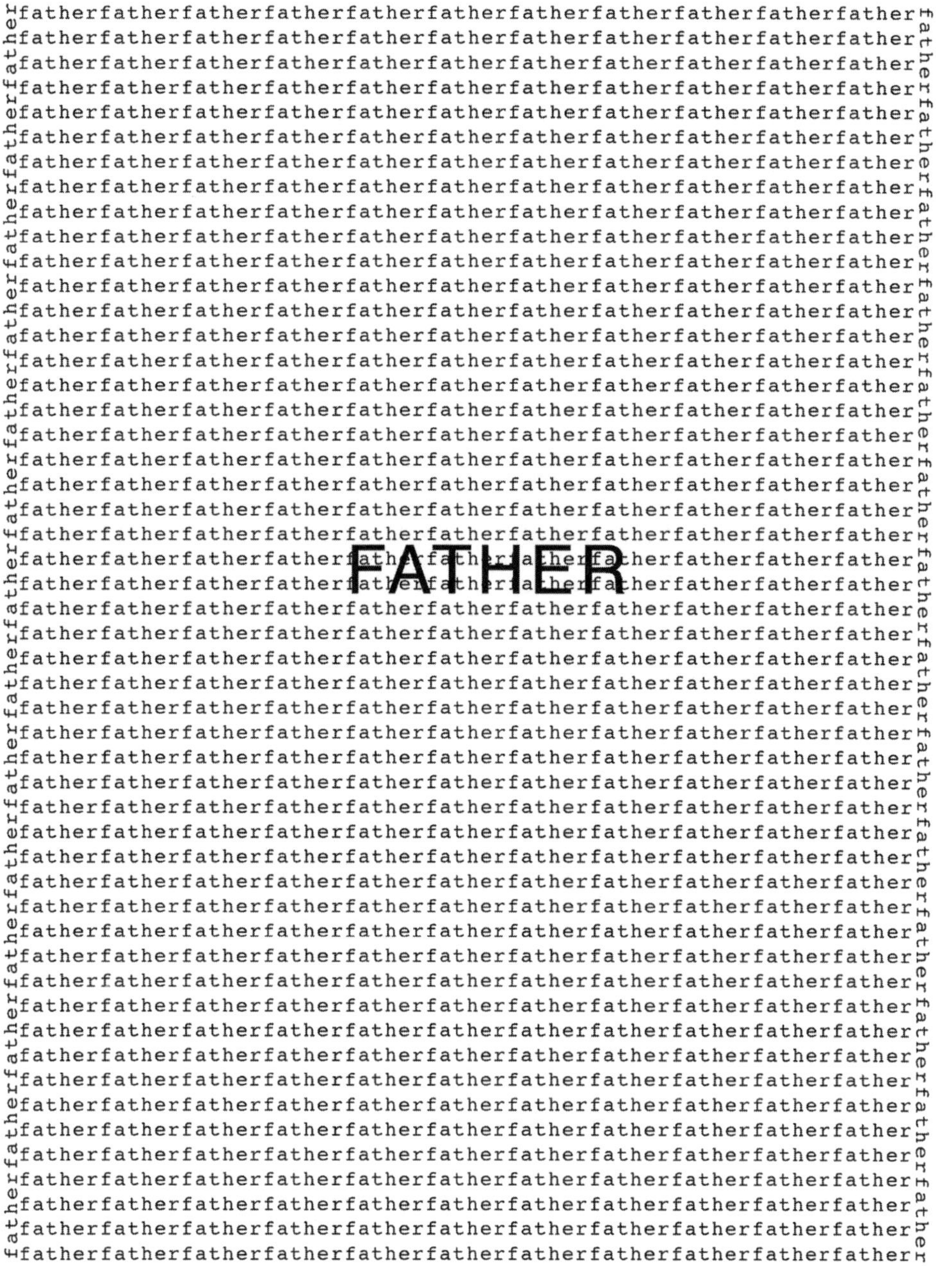

fatherfatherfatherfatherfatherfatherfatherfatherfatherfatherfather
fatherfatherfatherfatherfatherfatherfatherfatherfatherfatherfather
fatherfatherfatherfatherfatherfatherfatherfatherfatherfatherfather
fatherfatherfatherfatherfatherfatherfatherfatherfatherfatherfather
fatherfatherfatherfatherfatherfatherfatherfatherfatherfatherfather
fatherfatherfatherfatherfatherfatherfatherfatherfatherfatherfather
fatherfatherfatherfatherfatherfatherfatherfatherfatherfatherfather
fatherfatherfatherfatherfatherfatherfatherfatherfatherfatherfather
fatherfatherfatherfatherfatherfatherfatherfatherfatherfatherfather
fatherfatherfatherfatherfatherfatherfatherfatherfatherfatherfather
fatherfatherfatherfatherfatherfatherfatherfatherfatherfatherfather
fatherfatherfatherfatherfatherfatherfatherfatherfatherfatherfather
fatherfatherfatherfatherfatherfatherfatherfatherfatherfatherfather
fatherfatherfatherfatherfatherfatherfatherfatherfatherfatherfather
fatherfatherfatherfatherfatherfatherfatherfatherfatherfatherfather
fatherfatherfatherfatherfatherfatherfatherfatherfatherfatherfather
fatherfatherfatherfatherfatherfatherfatherfatherfatherfatherfather
fatherfatherfatherfatherfatherfatherfatherfatherfatherfatherfather
fatherfatherfatherfatherfatherfatherfatherfatherfatherfatherfather
fatherfatherfatherfatherfatherfatherfatherfatherfatherfatherfather
fatherfatherfatherfatherfatherfatherfatherfatherfatherfatherfather
fatherfatherfatherfatherfatherfatherfatherfatherfatherfatherfather

FATHER

fatherfatherfatherfatherfatherfatherfatherfatherfatherfatherfather
fatherfatherfatherfatherfatherfatherfatherfatherfatherfatherfather
fatherfatherfatherfatherfatherfatherfatherfatherfatherfatherfather
fatherfatherfatherfatherfatherfatherfatherfatherfatherfatherfather
fatherfatherfatherfatherfatherfatherfatherfatherfatherfatherfather
fatherfatherfatherfatherfatherfatherfatherfatherfatherfatherfather
fatherfatherfatherfatherfatherfatherfatherfatherfatherfatherfather
fatherfatherfatherfatherfatherfatherfatherfatherfatherfatherfather
fatherfatherfatherfatherfatherfatherfatherfatherfatherfatherfather
fatherfatherfatherfatherfatherfatherfatherfatherfatherfatherfather
fatherfatherfatherfatherfatherfatherfatherfatherfatherfatherfather
fatherfatherfatherfatherfatherfatherfatherfatherfatherfatherfather
fatherfatherfatherfatherfatherfatherfatherfatherfatherfatherfather
fatherfatherfatherfatherfatherfatherfatherfatherfatherfatherfather
fatherfatherfatherfatherfatherfatherfatherfatherfatherfatherfather
fatherfatherfatherfatherfatherfatherfatherfatherfatherfatherfather
fatherfatherfatherfatherfatherfatherfatherfatherfatherfatherfather
fatherfatherfatherfatherfatherfatherfatherfatherfatherfatherfather
fatherfatherfatherfatherfatherfatherfatherfatherfatherfatherfather
fatherfatherfatherfatherfatherfatherfatherfatherfatherfatherfather
fatherfatherfatherfatherfatherfatherfatherfatherfatherfatherfather
fatherfatherfatherfatherfatherfatherfatherfatherfatherfatherfather
fatherfatherfatherfatherfatherfatherfatherfatherfatherfatherfather
fatherfatherfatherfatherfatherfatherfatherfatherfatherfatherfather
fatherfatherfatherfatherfatherfatherfatherfatherfatherfatherfather
fatherfatherfatherfatherfatherfatherfatherfatherfatherfatherfather
fatherfatherfatherfatherfatherfatherfatherfatherfatherfatherfather
fatherfatherfatherfatherfatherfatherfatherfatherfatherfatherfather
fatherfatherfatherfatherfatherfatherfatherfatherfatherfatherfather

Actual size: 8 x 10

CHAPTER 10

be and being and been

be(e)-ing
after Beah Richards

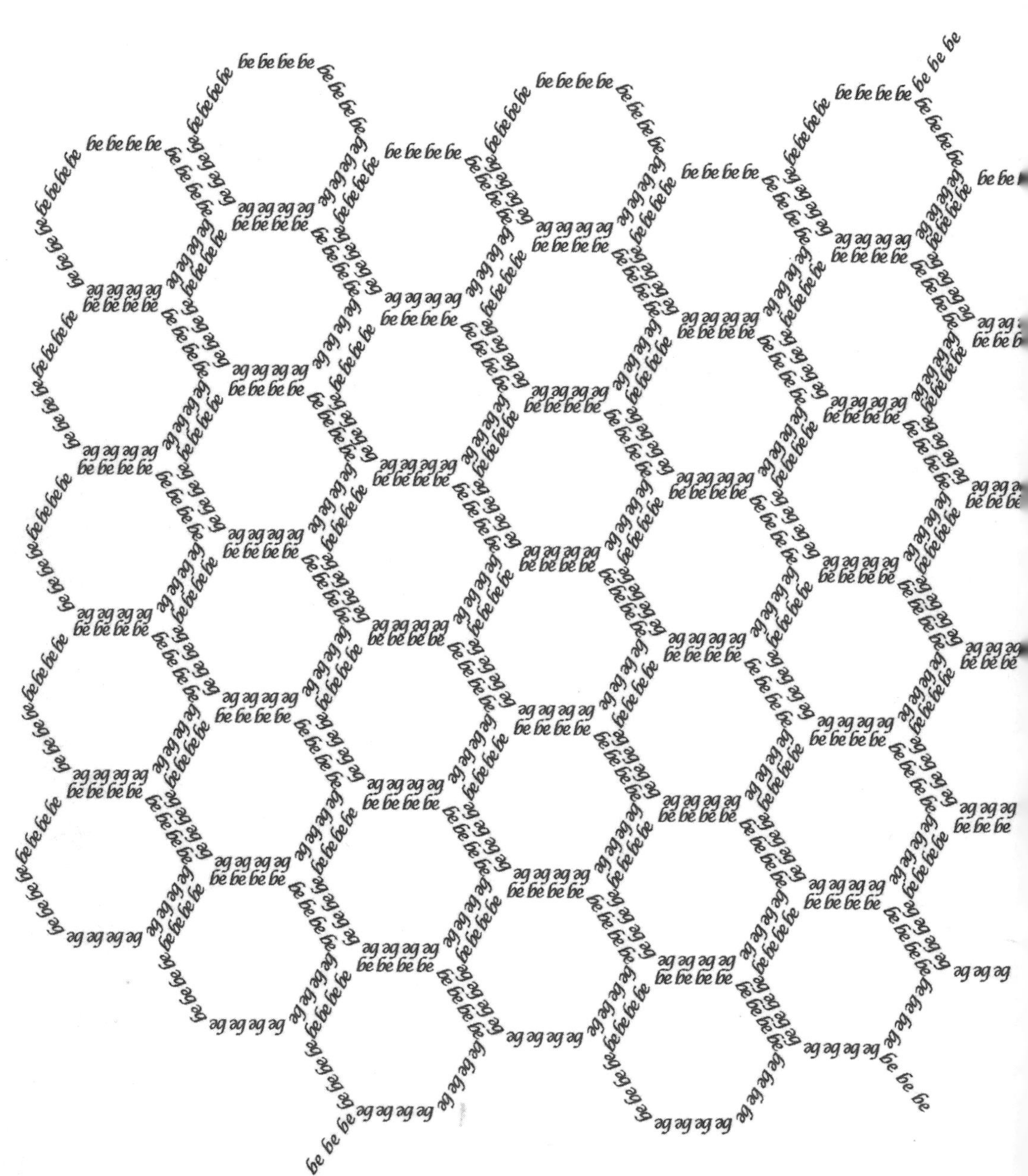

B	I	N	G	O
17	8	48	*Gertrude* at birth 58 and in death only	12
4	26	33	5	21
Nina aunt truthsayer 35 chile, look in my purse & bring me my cigarettes	42	FREE	10	68
16	59	*death don't* 13 *die*	54	*The Fox* manicured nails the finest finery 73 & every bit her stealthy namesake
29	five across five down 70 five children	2	46	11

Bingo Queen

for Gertrude "Nina, the Fox" Epps

be(e)-ing

continued. . .

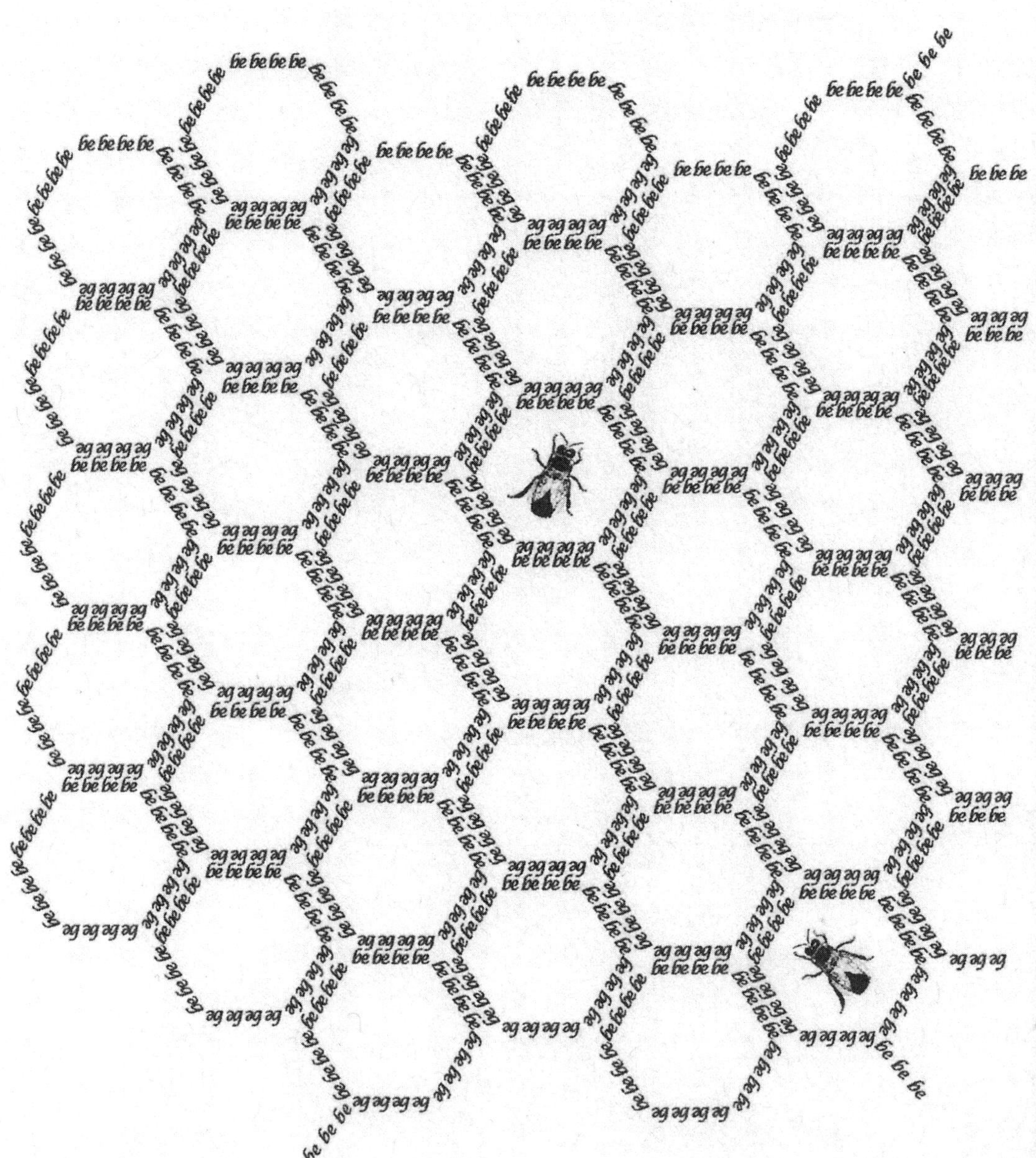

Some identification, please. . .

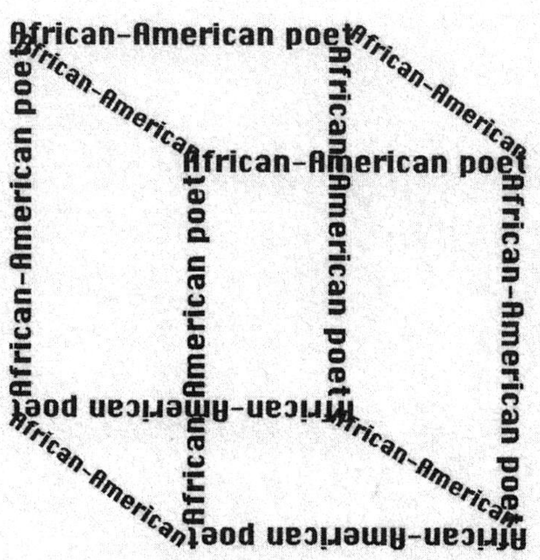
African-American poet
African-American
African-American
African-American poet
African-American poet
African-American poet
African-American poet
African-American poet
African-American poet
African-American
African-American
African-American poet

Fig. 1

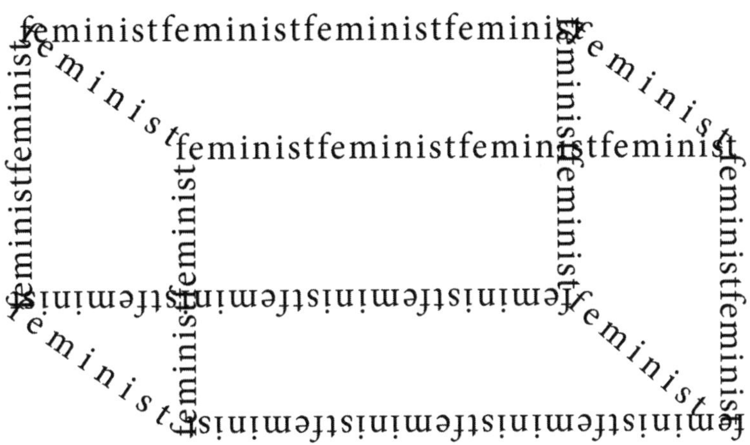
feministfeministfeministfeminist
feminist
feminist
feministfeminist
feministfeministfeministfeminist
feministfeminist
feminist
feministfeminist
feministfeministfeministfeminist
feministfeminist
feminist
feminist
feministfeministfeministfeminist

Fig. 2

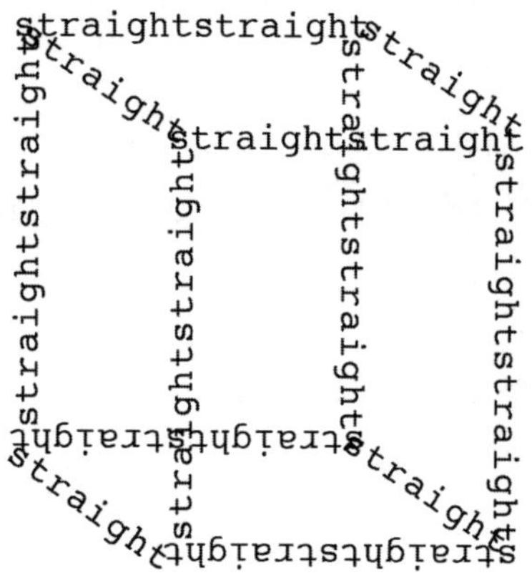
straightstraight
straight
straight
straightstraight
straightstraight
straightstraight
straightstraight
straightstraight
straightstraight
straight
straight
straightstraight

Fig. 3

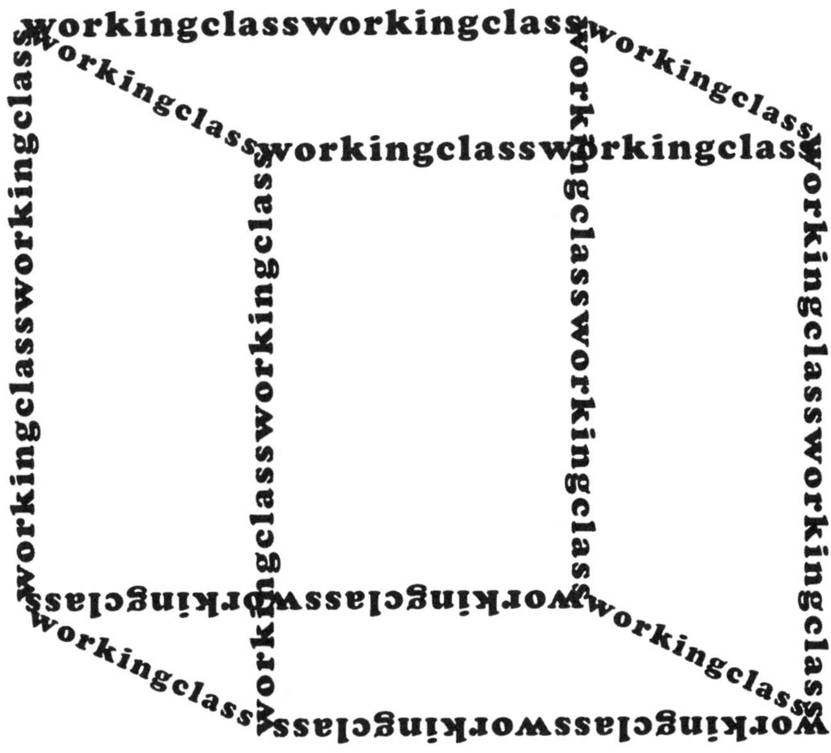
workingclassworkingclass
workingclass
workingclassworkingclass
workingclassworkingclass

Fig. 4

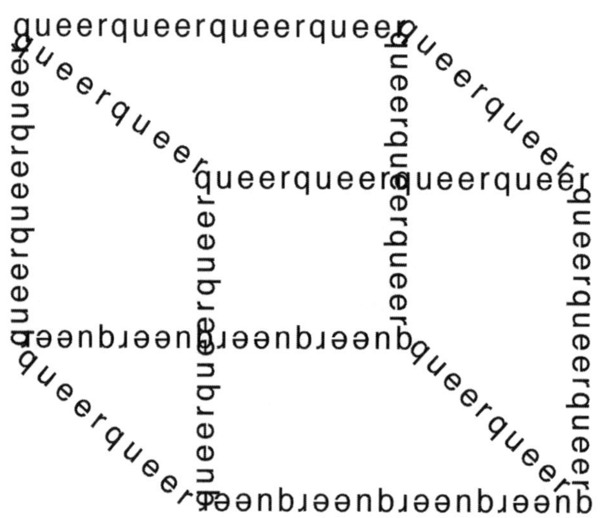

Fig. 5

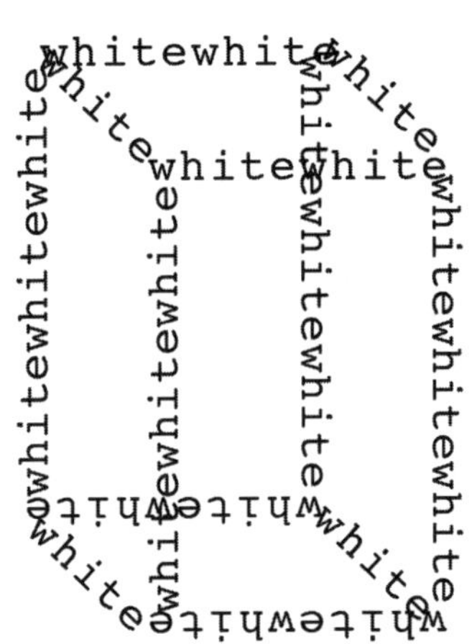

Fig. 6

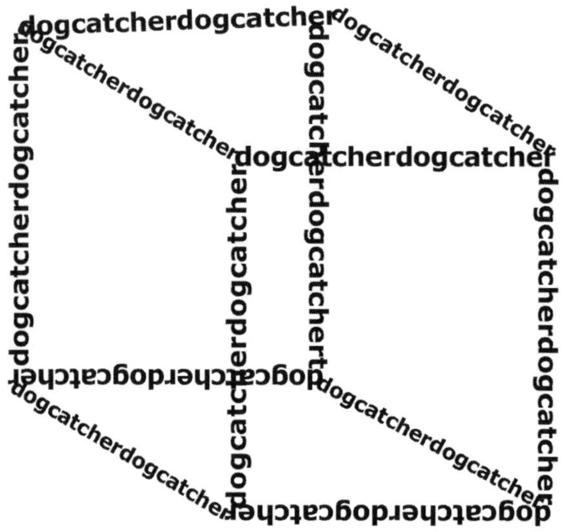
dogcatcherdogcatcher
dogcatcherdogcatcher
dogcatcherdogcatcher
dogcatcherdogcatcher
dogcatcherdogcatcher
dogcatcherdogcatcher
dogcatcherdogcatcher
dogcatcherdogcatcher
dogcatcherdogcatcher
dogcatcherdogcatcher
dogcatcherdogcatcher
dogcatcherdogcatcher

Fig. A

CHAPTER 11

C is the Color of Attention

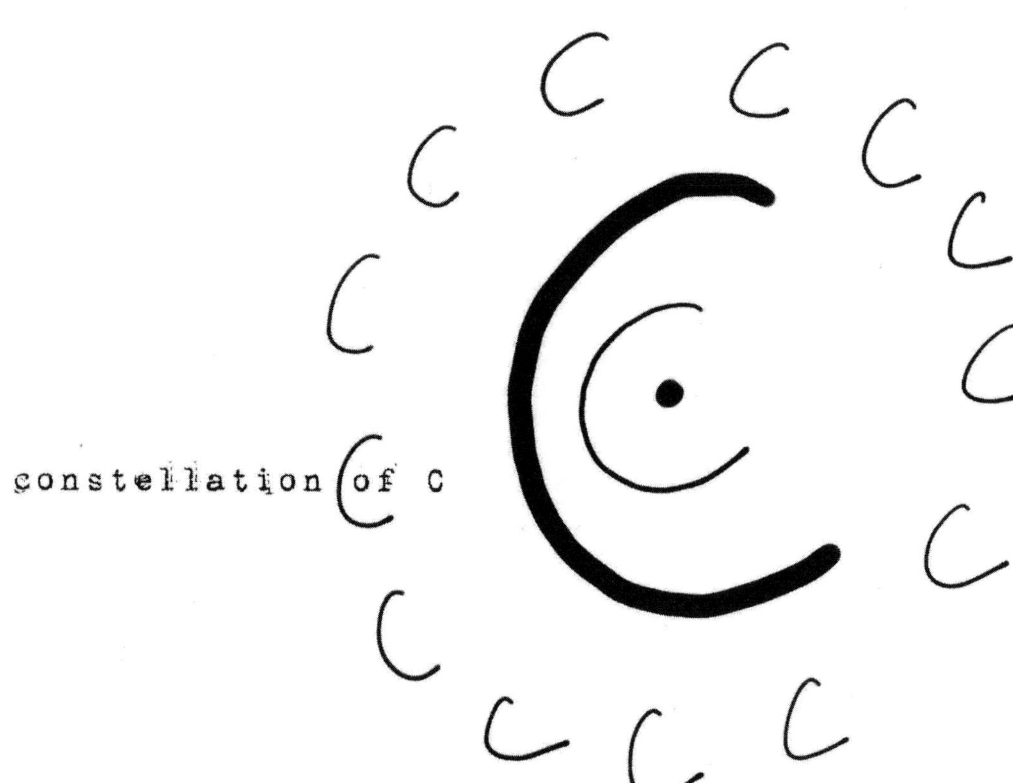
constellation of C

C is the Color of Attention or Abecedarianism's Architecture

I am learning to write the alphabet. Again.

They were miswritten in times before now.

They strained to conform.

Instruction led hand across languaged battlefields.

Japanese. Tibetan. English.

Calligraphy lessons to loosen the grip of a pen held too tightly.

I quit the uppercase *G* to reclaim my own authority.

Make a different *G*, a Vimala *G* composed from two sized *C*'s.

The literary archive and published facsimile allow for eavesdropping on past gestures.

The written by hand *could* be more true, more alive, living still.

Handwriting as flesh.

Reconfiguring my relationship to   letters.

The alphabet invests and animates words that

then make lines and expressive writing   connects,

communicates   and is an act   of paying attention.

C opens focus from the *cradle*

to the. . .   *C* being color,   being colored.

The letter *A* begins   it   and maybe   it's *C*'s ear.

C   as in   chant.

Copious, candle, confession, creation, confidence, causation, crave, collate, collaborate, cohort, calamity, Community. . .

I am relearning to write letters of an alphabet.

The letter *C* is present. *C* for consonance.

C for curse or collusion as *C* does with its sound of letters *K* or *S* most often.

Cloak and dagger. *C* makes a cup of coffee.

I observe *C* and fear for its openness or reluctance.

Womb??

I watch and study and practice on ruled and unruly paper.

I stalk *C* to its core. Minimalism mirrored in one-letter poems.

Braided cable like The Beatles sing "Let It Be, Let It Be"

made in the key of *C*.

Third letter of alphabetic system.

C's back rounds from an earlier version of a point stuck out.

Writing curves the body like *C*.

The practice of *C* produces constellated influence heretofore unknown.

Gathered up bones do music and shine like

Clifton (Lucille), *Coleman* (Wanda), *Coltrane* (Alice), *Cortez* (Jayne).

Scribbling scribed in poetry life.

All Californian caught tongue. Geographical trains of thought transmission

leave the station

and keep going on and on. . .

CHAPTER 12

eye of the be/holder (Take 2)

i

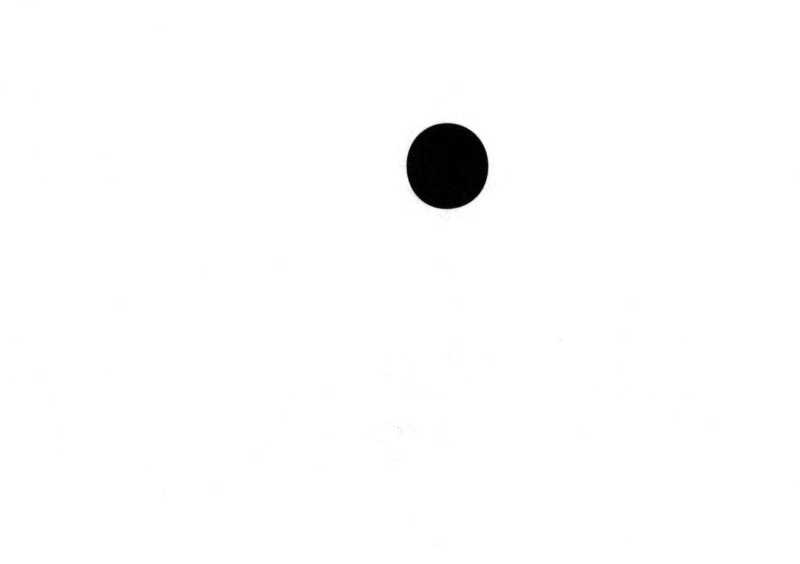

CHAPTER 13

Elliptical Moonbeams in Time: An Ethereal Wandering

What makes you feel like doin' stuff like that? (Quincy Jones). Dance wears down messy stress. Exchange economy. Ink to paper.

Often a road is not a road when looked at up close. See dirt path underneath. Ink and paper meet. Labor. Bare feet calloused.

Great hope is Spirit. Most frequent collaborator: dream bringer. Discourse of hovering/hunkering down.

Bees in bonnets unabsent. And o deer on forested front lawn. And manner of speaking in squirrely trees.

moon HERE is minus (isotope) *plus* light

Soul reconfiguration of field from cotton and tobacco into a Pacific open one. Now cage-less. Oppen's "Psalm" on stereo — elegance, grace, precision. Tattooed islands (like a Black Hawk one in Wisconsin) born then human connected dots. Demarcated brown flesh. Essentially all in the hearing.

Wings battered for love of leaps. . .the elevation viewed most contemporarily in b&w. A writing through cheesecloth; rigorous passage through death. Standup the stereotype. Watermelon out with the bathwater. Let us rejoice and be clean. Clean. Clear. Unambiguous but not unanimous.

Gray space between like some menu options are gray out and not available unless some other action takes place or the scene is changed. There is shielding the stain offers. The stain grows, becomes nuanced as if to color. Stained is permeation. With the -ed added, momentum leans toward addition.

Stained glass. The color spreads and becomes a part of glass. If Union says "possible."

Allowance. Mother and daughter and gray space occupies the space between. In between. From wings, it could favorably make a parachute. One with an imperceptible rip (or tear) in it. Faint sound of water flowing over rocks.

waning crescent. . .

The word "tower" is self-announcing stature I have an aversion to. Avert my eyes from a gaze that would stare. Ordinarily. But now its every mention renews my belief (and fear too perhaps a little) in destruction, in death. Maybe a conversion from "tower" to "butter" would be better, both getting to opposite endings naturally or the same unnaturally.

The me—my—I—ism of the Magic Carpet ride. Appropriately, weighted subjectivity. *Take my hand*, Thomas A. Dorsey wrote and sang. The "I" leads the way by way of "my" and ever on and under its own direction. Degrees of difference as breath shields and shades. The only "story" is the one never told or sold out.

Every 24 hours, singularity refuses to yield wholeness unless the whole is specified and/or sanctified. A groundless ground. Sun Ra would be an example. There is baptism, the washing and emerging anew ink stained black and back again.

Audio performances of some of the work in this book can be found at:
www.canarium.org/giovanni-singleton

ACKNOWLEDGMENTS

The author gratefully acknowledges the editors and curators of the following journals, anthologies, and exhibitions where these works, some in slightly different forms, first appeared:

Chain, *Aufgabe*, *Colorado Review*, *North American Review*, *Callaloo*, *Poetry*, *VOLT*, *Zen Monster*, *The Ecopoetry Anthology* (Trinity University Press), *Resisting Arrest: Poems to Stretch the Sky* (Jacar Press), *I'll Drown My Book: Conceptual Writing by Women* (Les Figues Press), *Hick Poetics* (Lost Roads Publishers), *Kindergarde: Avant-Garde Poems, Plays, Stories, and Songs for Children* (Black Raddish Books), *Among Margins: Critical & Lyrical Writing on Aesthetics* (Ricochet Editions), *What I Say: Innovative Poetry by Black Writers in America* (University of Alabama Press), *Quo Anima: Innovation and Spirituality in Contemporary Poetry* (Truman University Press), *2015 Best American Experimental Writing* (Wesleyan University Press), *Letters to the Future: BLACK Writing/Radical WRITING* (Kore Press), *First Annual Visual Poetry & Performance Festival* (San Francisco), and *Beyond Words: A Fusion of Poetry, Visual Art, and Jazz* (Smithsonian Institute's American Jazz Museum).

giovanni singleton, a native of Richmond, Virginia, is founding editor of *nocturnes (re)view* of the literary arts (nocturneseditions.com), a journal dedicated to experimental work of the African Diaspora and other contested spaces. Her debut poetry collection, *Ascension* (Counterpath Press), informed by the music and life of Alice Coltrane, was awarded the 81st California Book Award Gold Medal. She has received fellowships from the Squaw Valley Community of Writers Workshop, Cave Canem, Into the Fire: The Sun Celebrates Personal Writing, and the Napa Valley Writers Conference. singleton has taught at Sonoma State University, Naropa University, New Mexico State University, Cal Arts, California College of the Arts, and in museums and schools throughout the San Francisco Bay Area. She is the 2017-18 Holloway Lecturer in Poetry at the University of California, Berkeley where she also coordinates the Lunch Poems reading series.